Charting Commodity Market Price Behavior

By the author of—
Commodity Speculation—
With Profits In Mind
Commodity Solicitor's Examination
Commodity Trading Manual

Charting Commodity Market Price Behavior

L. Dee Belveal

Second Edition

DOW JONES-IRWIN
Homewood, Illinois 60430

© L. Dee Belveal, 1969 and 1985

This publication is designed to provide accurate and
authoritative information in regard to the subject matter
covered. It is sold with the understanding that the
publisher is not engaged in rendering legal, accounting, or
other professional service. If legal advice or other expert
assistance is required, the services of a competent
professional person should be sought.

*From a Declaration of Principles jointly adopted by a Committee
of the American Bar Association and a Committee of Publishers.*

ISBN 0-87094-651-X

Library of Congress Catalog Card No. 85-70189

Printed in the United States of America

1 2 3 4 5 6 7 8 9 0 K 2 1 0 9 8 7 6 5

Dedication
to Bill, and Don, and Bob
—with love and great pride.

Foreword

It is becoming increasingly clear that there is a large and growing segment of public traders who are approaching commodity speculation in a serious and scholarly fashion. There are still those who think hunches and lucky guesses will suffice in the quest for trading profits, but they will learn better in the school of bitter experience. For some, there is no other method of education.

But the serious-minded public speculator who has the time and the self-discipline to really qualify himself wants answers with which to avoid calamity. It is for him or her that this work is undertaken.

Much of the material in this book has been lifted directly from essays composed in answer to questions we have received in reader correspondence. A good many of those who have exchanged letters with us evidenced both surprise and appreciation for some comprehensive discussion of a problem point. So, what is helpful for a few may also have equal value for many. This, in any case, is the hope.

There is no gainsaying the fact that ignorance has been, and continues to be, a major element in much of the profits reaped by better-informed speculators and hedgers in commodity markets. The ill-informed, undisciplined, regularly over-extended public trader has long been the professional speculator's economic oyster. By the same token, hedgers have reason to give thanks for the gullibility the public has often demonstrated in buying risks that more astute commercial interests prudently seek to avoid. However, to admit the condition is not to condone it, nor to accept it as being in the best interests of either the market as an institution or its participants.

Commodity speculation is a valid and valuable economic activity. The current-pricing and value-forecasting functions that take place through trade in contracts for future delivery have accomplished great good for producers, processors, dealers, transporters, and consumers of the goods involved. Futures markets have brought a level of sophistication to decision making in production, standardization, distribution, and use-rationing that could not have been accomplished in any other fashion. Recurrent exertions in the area of government controls, price-fixing, etc., is eloquent evidence that the market invariably does the jobs better.

The business being transacted on commodity exchanges is public business. It has to do with the operational realities—and the risks—of producing, assembling, distributing, and putting values on the basic materials that feed, clothe, house, and otherwise sustain the population of this planet. It is far too important a function to relegate to a small coterie of professional traders and commercial interests.

The public has everything at stake in what transpires on the exchanges. Ergo, the public should have an important part in shaping the events that, in turn, shape the quality of our present and future existence.

Better information in the hands of more market participants will make speculation a more difficult business. When people stop making foolish mistakes, it takes a greater measure of skill to trade profitably against them. But there is a larger consideration.

The market is something less than a perfect institution. The quality of its performance is a direct reflection of the information, skills, and composite performance of those who are engaged in it. Better informed traders can only add up to a better informed market and an equivalent improvement in the reliability and social usefulness of the decisions the market reflects.

It is at least unfortunate that commodity markets have had the skimpy attention given them by business writers to this point. Bookstore shelves groan under the weight of innumerable, well-executed volumes dealing with virtually every other facet of economics. But the seeker of useful information about commodity markets can carry the full selection available home under one arm. This, in spite of the fact that we are dealing with trade volumes that far exceed those found in securities markets.

It takes a good deal of courage (or sheer insensitivity to criticism) to write in an area of this kind. Each individual tends to weave his own authoritarian robe out of personal experience. Experts seldom agree fully, and there is no target quite so inviting as a self-anointed expert who has the temerity to set his opinions down in a book and suggest that others adopt and follow them.

But let the barbs or the bouquets fly! This effort has succeeded in shining some light in the market where none shone before, and after more than 15 years of testing in the trade, it continues to be the bible on its subject matter! As the reader of these pages gleans valuable new insights into what makes a market behave as it does, both he and the market are well-served. Finally, if this book and its predecessor volumes stimulate other people of experience and knowledge to add to the literature in this woefully neglected field, then this might be the greatest benefit of all.

In any case, the information which follows has served your author and a growing cult of technical converts very well. Much of the material is not new but is rather a distillate of knowledge and/or suspicion that has grown out of watching events repeatedly develop from a given set of conditions. It is always dangerous to pursue the rationale of "after that, therefore because of that." In doing so, we may ascribe observed events to all of the wrong causes and badly delude ourselves in the process. Still, a good deal of technical market analysis must be judgmental. It is just not possible to know what prompts the full mix of human activities that produces a composite market effect. The market doctor must become adept in appraising conditions, noting symptoms, and translating it all into a projection of underlying strengths and weaknesses. It's a practice in behavioral psychology, as well as an exercise in economic analysis.

Those who learn to do it well can expect to build up some very impressive bank accounts.

In acknowledging the indispensable assistance from others who played a vital role in bringing this book into existence, a long list of members and officers of the Chicago Board of Trade (CBOT) must head the roster. Over a period of many years, this organization has given the author full access to information and records that provide a veritable gold mine for research. Through the patient and intelligent assistance of Warren W. Lebeck, former executive vice president and secretary of the board, it was possible to find information—or individuals in the exchange membership and staff who possessed information—on every facet of market mechanics and theory.

By virtue of enjoying the courtesy of the trading floors of most of the exchanges, it has been possible to research trader reactions at the very vortex of the action: standing in the pits and watching the events described in this book unfold.

Personal thanks must be given to William J. Mallers, former chairman of the CBOT board of directors and a professional speculator. His suggestions and criticisms did much to strengthen several areas of the final manuscript, as well as to keep explanations closely tied to market realities.

Paul F. McGuire, holder of a doctorate in economics and a professional speculator, is another individual whose wealth of experience and technical competence was extensively drawn on in the full course of this work.

Some of the other helpers in this project, in no particular order of their contributions to the final result, are:

Conrad Leslie, crop forecaster
Francis D. Wolfe, broker/trader
Michael H. Helberg, trader

C. W. Schultz, Jr., Kohlmeyer & Co.
Alfred H. Gruetzmacher, broker
Bernard P. Carey, trader
Joseph J. Kane, broker

We must also acknowledge the usefulness of a wide assortment of market publications that were provided by more than a dozen of the major brokerage firms. Also, our deep appreciation for literally scores of market advisory letters and special bulletins that emanated from commission houses of all sizes and areas of interest. Continuing analyses of such variety of market opinions have vastly widened the original perspective of this work. Even though such a wealth of sources will never reflect agreement, their disparities of opinion can be most instructive to the scholarly observer.

As a practical matter, the training of a market participant is accomplished under a large and ever-changing group of "professors." Each commodity position should add something to the fund of knowledge with which a trader faces the next risk situation. Each conversation with another trader should add a new idea or bring an existing idea into closer, more useful focus.

It is notable that, while this book deals with things long felt to be almost the exclusive domain of the professionals in the market, there was never a word of opposition to its publication. Such differences of opinion as arose (and there were many) related to presentation, accuracy of example, or ancillary quarrels about validity or usefulness to the reader. From this it can only be seen that upgrading the informational tools of the public trader was a project welcomed by the vast majority of the practicing professionals, even though the availability of this book is dramatically changing the character of commodity trading.

In short, they neither need nor seek the advantage inherent in going up against an uninformed group of competitors. The clear concensus is that the more market information there is available to everyone, the better it will be for the market—and for all those who use it.

It should surprise no one to learn that this book is not unanimously concurred in, even by those who had important roles in developing it. Attitudes vary widely on the matters treated in these pages. To the hard-core fundamentalist, charts may be considered an empty exercise—nearly, or totally, useless. At the other extreme, there are those who put almost boundless faith in their charts—as the best available barometers of upcoming market weather. Taking the middle-ground between these extremes of viewpoint may have succeeded in satisfying no one. However, we subscribe to an approach that contains parts of the persuasions of each camp and one that has clearly withstood the tests of time and critical examination.

Rely on this volume to help you avoid the pitfalls that usually lurk in any pat procedure that calls for putting all of one's eggs in any single basket.

The opinions expressed herein are those of the author and may or may not be shared by his acknowledged mentors. To the extent this work proves useful, its value must be attributed to many. If it falls short of expectations, the responsibility rests exclusively with the writer.

L. Dee Belveal

Preface

Commodity trading is not nearly as difficult or as dangerous as some of its uninformed critics would have you believe. It is, beyond any possible argument, far less complex and a good deal safer than trading stocks for price appreciation, for example. Additionally, the smaller margins required in commodity speculation offer 8 to 10 times the return on dollars used in commodity markets, as compared to those committed in securities. And most importantly, there is no such thing as an insider in the commodity markets; all traders must make their judgments from essentially the same information reservoir. If an individual elects to not use the data that exists to guide him, that is his decision and his risk.

For the person who will take the time and expend the effort required under the heading of "market homework," there is probably no other area in the entire economic scene that can equal the profit potentials of professional speculation. Also, it is reassuring to note, it is an activity in which a well-informed newcomer has every bit as much opportunity to succeed as the much-vaunted old-timer. Perhaps the newcomer has an advantage in that he doesn't have to unlearn a lifetime's accumulation of misleading information and poor trading practices that abounded in earlier times, when commodity speculation was considered sinful at best and, at worst, a threat to the national morals and well-being.

At this writing, the mechanics of trade and the economic effects that arise from speculation on organized commodity exchanges are under the most searching examination ever accorded the topics. An impressive list of major universities are currently putting heavy emphasis on speculation in their business courses. Other distinguished institutions are conducting seminars in speculation at the graduate level and pursuing research into the principles and results of organized trading in futures contracts.

Marketing scholars have long understood—and an increasing group of public and private authorities are coming to learn—that there is no more efficient or equitable way to discover prices than through the open-auction machinery of the free market. Neither federal edict nor the electronic cerebrations of a computer is entirely trustworthy, especially when it comes to mediating the highly vested interests of producers and consumers. In either case, selected experts develop the policies or program the machines, and the results are rarely free of at least a taint of favoritism for either the buyers or the sellers.

A free market functions under no such handicap. Operating under regulations that protect everyone from the dangers of undue influence by large interests, or manipulation by crooks, the market can be confidently trusted to tell it like it is. Supply and demand stand eyeball-to-eyeball in the pits and rings, in the form of orders to buy and sell for future delivery. Price fluctuations of small or large proportions measure the ongoing tides of economic battle, as sellers fight for high prices and buyers strive to make lower prices prevail.

To anyone who has witnessed or taken part in the trading spectacle, it is obvious that the system is something less than a perfect device for transferring goods, and the risks that ownership of those goods entails. But, for all of its admitted shortcomings, the open auction still stands as the most reliable, most efficient, most equitable means for dealing in—and pricing—the raw materials with which to feed, clothe, house, and otherwise sustain the world's population. Time and new technology may some day develop a better way, but it does not now exist.

Speculation has only recently begun to emerge from under the clouds of distrust that have hung over it for generations. Ignorance of both the marketplace and the functions of those who deal in it have perpetuated an endless series of attacks against commodity trading that have only lately begun to subside. The zenith of ignorant and baseless calumny was reached by a former president of the United States, who termed speculators in commodities "merchants of human misery."

A modicum of digging into the role of the marketplace and of its speculators would have shown even this woefully uninformed critic that, rather than dealers in hunger and privation, speculators are the indispensable middlemen in financing, assembling, and distributing the basic elements of our world-renowned affluence. That speculators seek profits from their activities is no more detractive of them than is, let us say, the fact that doctors, lawyers, and clergymen expect payment for their services. Ours is essentially an economic society, and profit (or payment for goods and services) can't be defined as a dirty word as long as it remains so.

In defense of the critics of the marketplace, however, it must be admitted that the exchanges themselves have done far too little in the area of public information. Considering that the value of only the grain contracts traded on the Chicago Board of Trade exceed a trillion dollars per year, it is at least remarkable that almost any medium-sized consumer-goods manufacturer spends more money annually promoting his merchandise than the world's largest agricultural commodity exchange spends telling its story and explaining its economic function to the public! It is axiomatic that people tend to distrust anything they don't understand, and lack of understanding has plagued commodity exchanges like no other institutions on earth.

The underlying reason can certainly not be attributed to a lack of interest on the part of the financial audience. When *Commodity Speculation* first came into print some 18 years ago, a projected two-years supply of the book sold out in just slightly less than six months! And sales of the title continue to grow, spurred by brokerage house recommendations and proliferating display in the nation's bookstores.

Along with the gratifying volume of sales that the speculation book continued to show, another effect was seen. A deluge of letters began that has not slowed yet. Readers of the first volume continued to shower your author with market questions that, while both answerable and deserving of answers, nevertheless constituted an extremely time-consuming correspondence load. The vast majority of such letters contained questions that relate primarily to the technical side of the market. Most such letters were answered—and this book constituted an even more extensive reply to all those who wrote and to others who intended to write but didn't.

The reader is urged to study this work in connection with the *Speculation* volume. There is nothing in this book that is inconsistent with the trading principles detailed in its predecessor publication. Quite the contrary, concepts set down in both augment each other constantly. Much if not all of the contents of *Commodity Speculation* could have been reprinted in this volume—and would have been, were it not for the fear of pressing the reader beyond his limits of endurance with such extensive repetition.

It was ultimately decided to hold this work exclusively to the matters of technical market concern. In doing so, there is no choice except to assume that you have read *Commodity Speculation* or that you have a good working knowledge of how a market functions. Unless one of these assumptions is correct, much of the material between these covers is going to be either lost on you—or downright confusing.

The reader should be prepared to encounter some repetitions herein. This work has been prepared with the intention of making each chapter as nearly a self-sufficient monograph on its topic as reasonable space limitations permit. As a consequence, certain basic rules or applications will appear in more than one location. By doing so, we hope the usefulness of the volume will be enhanced and that using it will require minimal reliance on the index.

L. D. B.

Contents

Schedule of Charts

1

In Defense of Clear Language

A recurrent debate has ensued with some of the collaborators and interim reviewers of this manuscript with regard to the choice of language used to describe certain market phenomena. To many market people, using the terminology of the trading floor seems to invite misunderstanding and criticism from the uninitiated. Indeed it may—but the alternative is to clothe matters that deserve the utmost clarity in semantic ruffles that can only stand between the reader and the text.

First on the list of words that are likely to cause trouble is *scalper*.

Be Thankful for Scalpers

At the vortex of every market, there must be individuals who are willing to trade for small profit opportunities. If there were no scalpers (the securities markets call them *specialists*, but they fulfill the same function), there would certainly be a great loss in market liquidity. Without liquidity, the seller finds he must often accept bids that are well below "equilibrium." The buyer in a poorly scalped market discovers that the price at which he can do business likewise tends to be higher than it should be.

The pit scalper performs an indispensable service for both buyers and sellers in affording both the best possible conditions under which to obtain or dispose of holdings. It is, of course, regrettable that scalper conjures up a negative impression in the minds of the uninformed. The

1

impression is totally undeserved. But avoiding the term is not likely to contribute much to improved understanding of the scalper's function and value. So we have used the label wherever it applies to pit activities involving short-term purchases and sales on the part of professional traders. It is an accurate designation and a highly useful, one-word description of a particular kind of market function. If there are those who don't understand it, then it is they who should undertake to expand their market vocabulary.

Events Cause Squeezes

Squeeze is another term that raises the hackles of a group of sensitive traders. The argument against the word rests mainly on the fear that members of the public or officials in the regulatory agencies might impute some kind of wrong-doing to those who are on the profitable side of a squeeze.

Again, the word is accurate, perfectly understandable, and no more an invitation to odium than scalper is. In the lexicon in which this book is written, a squeeze is any market situation in which sharply rising or falling prices make offset mandatory for a group of position-holders who are on the losing side of the contract. A market squeeze requires no *"engineers."* It can result from a government crop report or a longshoreman's strike. A dry five-day forecast or a much-needed rainstorm can, each in its time, set off a march to higher or lower prices in the affected contracts; and when they do, what simpler or more useful descriptive term than squeeze can we hope to find?

In the same vein, there were some strident objections raised to textual passages that refer to traders being *chased out* of their positions in the face of rising or falling prices. It would be possible to convey the same thought by saying that "disadvantaged position holders elected to offset at market prices rather than remain vulnerable to further price adversity." But your author prefers saying that the losers are chased out—and this is the way every floor trader is most likely to state it, also.

Market Language Is Functional

There are other specific examples that could be added to the list of "bad words," but the essential point should be sufficiently made with the three terms discussed above. Giving a literal meaning to professional idiom is simply absurd: A scalper is about as likely to take a scalp as a mule skinner is to skin a mule. But, to abandon the colorful and functional argot that has surrounded the markets for generations would be unthinkable, even if it were possible. The trading fraternity has its time-honored vernacular, and this book is written about and for traders. It is, for this reason, written in language they are most likely to understand with a minimum of pondering over abstruse meanings.

If, in choosing this course, we have injured the sensibilities or marred the image of either the traders or the exchanges, our apology is sincerely offered.

It has been the author's constant endeavor to present both markets and traders in the most accurate light possible. The institution of commodity speculation needs no defense. It stands in the forefront of activities that serve the most basic requirements of the human family. The men and women who conduct the markets and participate in trade need no special pleading, either. They perform their functions and undertake their risks with efficiency and fortitude that deserves the utmost commendation from all of their beneficiaries on the outside.

2

Introduction to Technical Trading

Life for a commodity speculator would be much simpler if markets responded consistently—and exclusively—to the measurable realities of supply and demand. But supply and demand are not the only elements that must be considered in the trader's appraisal of his prospects for success in a given market position.

Unforeseen events that go under the esoteric heading of *technical factors* often intervene, to the consternation and financial disadvantage of those who failed to foresee the possibility of a sharp and perhaps calamitous reversal in prices. It is inconceivable that anyone who has had even the most modest exposure to either the securities or commodities markets can be a stranger to the term *technical correction*. However, understanding of the technical side of the market is far less widespread than the recurrent use of the term would seem to indicate.

Most people tend to attribute any market event that they can't ascribe to palpable changes in supply/demand equilibrium to technical causes. While they may be correct in their assignment of the label, it would be even more helpful if they understood the interrelated considerations that triggered the given reaction, or better yet, if the situation could have been identified beforehand—and exploited!

Nearly everyone is able to understand the basic relationship of supply and demand to the function of pricing in the marketplace. Most everyone can appreciate the fact that if a given free-market society consumes a given quantity of a commodity over a specified period of time—and provided consumption and production proceed more or less equally through the period involved—the commodity will find a price level that it will theoretically maintain quite consistently. An increase in production will create a marginal surplus, with the result that the price will fall somewhat. A drop in production will result in a relatively increased shortage and will be reflected in a price increase.

Supply/Demand Usually Sets Trends

On organized commodity exchanges, however, the cause/effect relationship of supply/demand equilibrium on prices, although of great importance, is not the *only* consideration the trader must weigh in forecasting the probable course of prices, or in anticipating interim behavior of prices, even though they do continue to *trend* toward his forecasted ob-

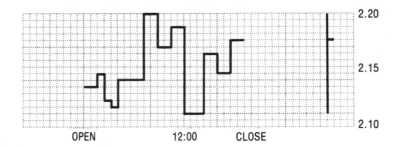

Chart 2-1

The constant ebb and flow of buying and selling pressures can trace out a price graph in each session that is every bit as complex—and often as significant—as the plottings of daily bars over longer periods of time. Pit scalpers and day traders hope to profit by selling and buying on the dips and bulges that occur within the daily trading range.

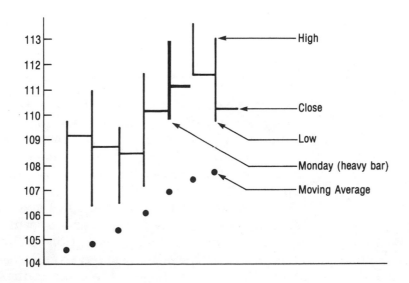

Chart 2-2

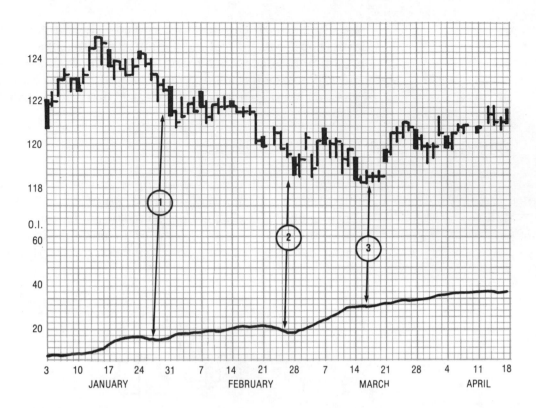

Chart 2-3

Addition of open-interest data vastly increases the amount of information one can glean from a chart. Most importantly, it often answers the question, "Are the traders willing to *follow* prices higher or lower, or does price movement in a given direction result in shrinking particpation in the contract?"

In the above chart, both the January and February dips brought noticeable offsetting from *both* longs and shorts: (1) and (2).

It was not until after the contract had successfully withstood the March test at 118 (3) that both sides visibly heaved a sigh of relief—and open-interest clearly documents their willingness to follow price into higher ground.

Open interest is usually reflected in millions of bushels in grains and is shown in contracts in other commodity categories. Volume is ordinarily handled in the same fashion.

jective. An examination of the simplest daily bar chart will demonstrate that price progression is rarely an unbroken line to a higher or lower level. While the *trend* of prices may be clearly higher or lower, the precise route followed is an endless succession of zigzags. It is this fluctuative characteristic in price behavior that we will be dealing with in this volume.

The vast majority of commodity traders consider themselves reasonably competent in forecasting the results of an increase or decrease in production, provided consumption can be expected to maintain a degree of consistency. An even larger majority of commodity traders feel extremely inadequate in attempting to measure the vulnerability of a

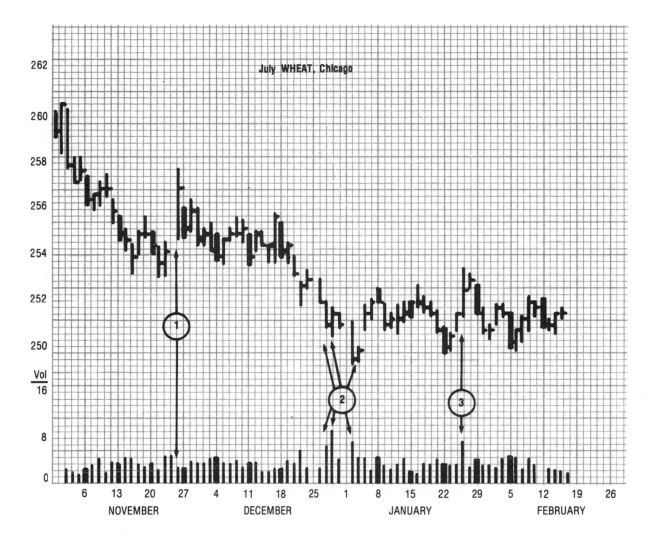

Chart 2-4

The principal value of trade-volume data is in gauging the urgency with which losers want out of the contract, whether at *higher* or *lower* prices.

(1) tells us that the disadvantaged short-holders didn't take the sharp run-up on Friday, November 24, very seriously. In spite of more than 2 cent impairment, they stood their ground.

It was a different story on December 27 and 28, (2). When the contract broke under 252, the longs began leaving in droves! A near-repeat took place on January 2, when the price went through the 250 level.

(3) A small flurry of weak-handed, short offsetting was a feature of the January 25 session. For the most part, however, the short-holders reflected tremendous confidence in the profit potentials of the position they occupied throughout this period.

given price level to the impact of a technical *reversal* or *correction*. While technical considerations are not nearly as measurable as the fundamentals of supply and demand, they are nonetheless sufficiently susceptible to anticipation as to give the market technician a better-than-

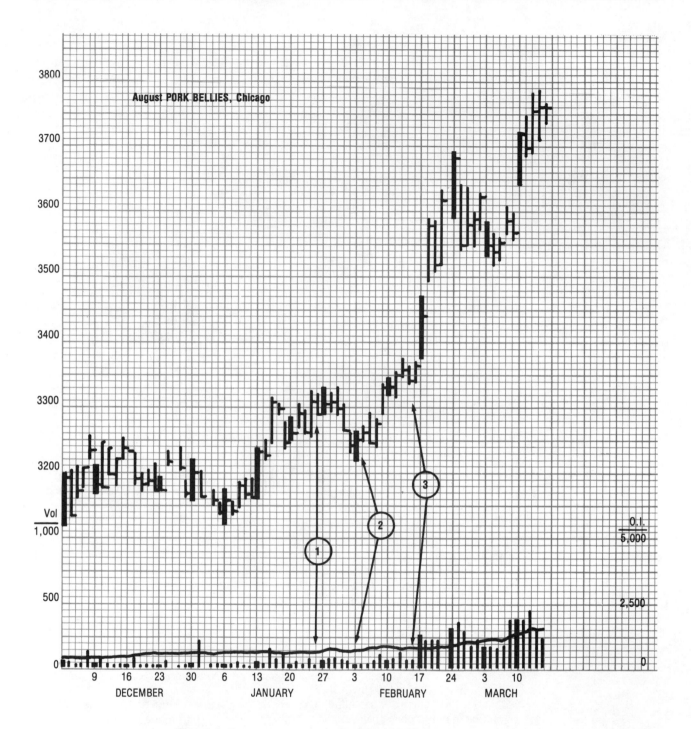

Chart 2-5

A chart that provides visual indices to price, volume and open-interest offers a quality of market perspective that none of the indicators, by itself, can convey.

The little bulge in volume and open-interest that came in connection with the 3300 level in January, (1), should have alerted chart-followers to what was coming. Then, when there was no response to the February 3 dip (2), and both volume and open-interest began "following price uphill" at mid-month (3), the stage was set for a major breakout.

even chance at forecasting both the timing and the extent of a technical phenomenon. In making such judgments, there are three essential points of reference.

1. Price patterns as reflected by standard charting procedures.
2. Open-interest in the commodity and in individual contracts as reported by the several exchanges and/or the Commodity Futures Trading Commission (CFTC).
3. Trading volume on a daily and/or weekly basis as reported by the individual exchanges and/or the CFTC.

Don't Overlook Trade Mix

Additionally, the market technician must concern himself with the trading *mix*. He must be constantly aware of the proportion of large traders, commercial hedgers, and small public traders, all of whom constitute the sum total of hands holding open positions in the market.

Each of these categories of traders has different and quite predictable behavioral characteristics. This is to say that success in the form of profits, or disappointments in the form of losses, will elicit different responses from these three important categories of market participants. The market technician must understand the personalities of his competition if he is to understand the technical personality of the market in which he is trading. Doing so—to repeat for emphasis—is not as difficult as it might appear on the surface.

Commodity speculation is, by its very nature, an exercise in risks. Vagaries of weather and the fickleness of international trading activities confront commodity speculators with a wealth of opportunities for making wrong judgments. A crop may fail or produce a bumper harvest; a large foreign customer may decide to fill its needs for a given commodity elsewhere, or it may double its orders in any given year. It is the speculator's constant challenge to foresee these events before they occur or, at the very least, be in a position to capitalize on them as soon as they are known. The successful speculator's ability to perform this admittedly difficult task is attested to in the size of his bank account.

When it comes to the behavior patterns of large groups of traders in the market, however, a much greater degree of predictability exists. We have a wealth of historical evidence to draw on. In short, we can be quite sure that the weak-handed public trader will be content with small profits but will usually stay around to sustain substantially larger losses. We can depend on the well-financed professional speculator to reflect a good deal of self-discipline and tenacity in the face of adversity, but he will also press his advantage aggressively to take the maximum profit out of a winning position.

We can safely assume that commercial hedging interests are only peripherally concerned with flat price levels themselves, since the market activities of hedgers almost invariably relate to price differentials

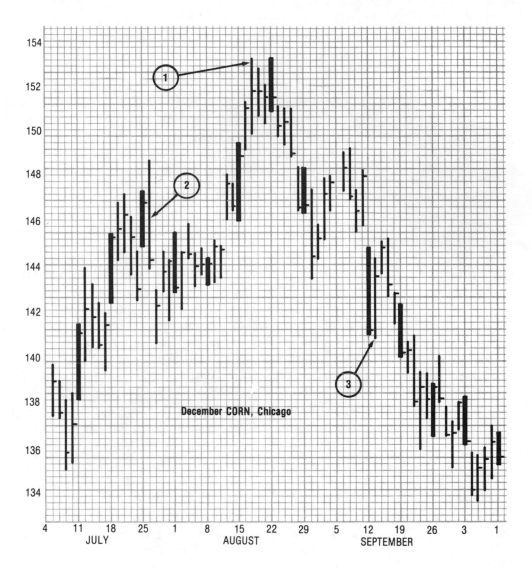

Chart 2-6

Occasionally we may find classical price patterns in commodities that seem to follow all of the interpretive rules in common usage. For example, this corn chart shows an excellent *head and shoulders*—but it made its top without the so-called key-reversal tracing and fooled a lot of chart analysts in the process. Those who are inclined to trust double-tops had a good one here (1), at 153 ⅜.

Volume and open-interest behavior were flying warning flags from 150, up. July 26 (2) and September 13 (3) were highly effective traps, but traders who relied on price data alone were deprived of the warnings that volume and open-interest data were giving.

---

between the cash product and the futures contracts, which will be the cash product equivalent at some point in near or distant time.

Our points of reference for these trader characteristics extend over more than 100 years of organized futures trading in the United States, and from these past events, we can draw incisive and useful conclusions about the shape of things to come.

Over the past 20 years your author has received more correspondence seeking answers to technical market behavior than any other single topic. A majority of the writers have made some direct reference to a chart pattern which reflected a price trend that the writer earnestly hoped would continue. It is consistent experience that most such correspondence relates to positions already held, rather than positions under contemplation. For the most part, also, the inquiring trader tends to limit his viewpoint to the matter of price alone, ignoring such things as trading volume, open interest, and makeup of the groups holding long and short positions in the given contract or commodity. To follow such a procedure is roughly approximate to a doctor relying on a pulse count alone as a measurement of his patient's total health.

The author has stated elsewhere, and must repeat, that the usual bar chart, which reflects daily price, trading-ranges, and market closes, is only slightly better than random determination in forecasting *medium-term price direction*. However, this should not be taken to mean that *all charts* are without value. Nothing could be further from the truth.

Technical Analysis Is for Short Term

There may be no better—and there is certainly no easier—way to analyze the health of a market than through the use of charts. While none of the individual technical indicators meet the test for making medium-term or long-range price projections, they are priceless when used *in combination* as dependable and consistent warning signs to alert you against *short-term* hazards which may lurk on the road ahead.

As a consequence, it is suggested that the reader respect his charts for the job that they *can* do, while remaining mindful of the hazards of putting too much confidence in charts in areas in which their reliability is at least subject to serious question. In pursuing this course, your author will certainly agitate those aficionados of charting who insist that each pennant, flag, saucer, and gap has a meaning of its own that can be followed with something like impunity. At the same time, no doubt, your author will incur some measure of wrath from certain academicians who hold that charting falls in about the same area of nonscience as tea-leaf-reading or ouija-board manipulation.

Nonetheless, a great deal of speculative experience and a continuing involvement in scholarly research leads to the firm conclusion that, limited though they are, charts provide the best readily available key to the technical health of the market. On this basis it is my advice, and it has been my practice, to use charts to the extent that they enhance speculative efficiency. To do otherwise would be to abandon one of the most useful tools we have available in an area where tools of any kind are altogether too scarce.

3

Using Past Information to Forecast the Future

One of the major obstacles the average trader has encountered in his efforts to analyze the continuing technical condition of the commodity markets has been the delays or sheer difficulty in obtaining the data required for the task. Trading volume information, for example, is only released during the trading session by two of our American commodity exchanges. The Chicago Mercantile Exchange and the New York Mercantile Exchange both process transaction slips throughout the trading session and provide trading volume estimates on a contract-by-contract basis at 30-minute intervals within the trading period. The other commodity exchanges, at this writing, wait until the end of the session, after which all of the transactions are recapped and one total trading volume figure is released for each contract, covering the entire session.

Hard-to-Get Information

With respect to open-interest, none of the American commodity exchanges makes an attempt to provide intra-session adjustments. Only after each session has ended is the number of contracts held open adjusted upward or downward to reflect a numerical increase or decrease in trade holdings during the market day being reported. These numbers are usually available the *second* morning through such publications as *The Wall Street Journal, New York Journal of Commerce,* and a few dailies, and the *next morning* from the individual exchanges themselves.

12

The numbers may also be available from a designated market information line into each exchange, as well as being carried on the respective exchange ticker tapes that go into brokerage offices, etc.

Only prices are provided on a minute-by-minute basis from all exchanges as trade progresses.

The proportion of long and short holdings in the hands of small and large speculators and hedgers is even less timely. The Commodity Futures Trading Commission issues a "Commitments of Traders" report at monthly intervals. Each report is distributed about the 10th of each month, and reflects positions held at the end of the preceding month. Needless to say, the mix of position holdings as reflected in the CFTC report can have already changed substantially by the time the report gets into the hands of those who will use it. It is still well worth the $36 per year that CFTC charges for it, for anyone who trades.

Increasing public involvement in the commodity markets is bringing additional pressure for better and more timely market information. But much improvement is still required before the commodity trader will have anything approaching the wealth of statistical information that is constantly raining down in the securities markets. The period required to accomplish this informational upgrading will largely depend on how loudly—and how often—commodity traders voice their needs to those in authority in the exchanges and in departments of government, especially the Commodity Futures Trading Commission and pertinent congressional bodies with responsibilities in the financial sector.

The computer-generated information revolution is vastly increasing the amount of data available to anyone who wishes to avail himself of such an avalanche of minutiae. The last bastion of inflexibility, however, seems to be those who offer a weekly package of charts to their subscribers. For the most part, they are turning out essentially the same data as always: daily-price bar charts, along with composite totals reflecting trading volume and open-interest in the various commodity classifications. Their persistence in holding to this practice is all the evidence we need to know that their business is *selling charts*—not *trading the markets!*

General Information Won't Suffice

A trader doesn't take a position in "corn." He takes a position in one or more of the five corn maturities that are constantly open for trading. To know that there are now some 700 million bushels of corn futures open—and that daily volume in corn futures is averaging about 160 million bushels—may be all a price-shooter needs to see. The numbers seem to assure a high degree of liquidity in the market, if this is the only concern.

However, for the public trader who is considering a new position in corn, or enlargement or liquidation of an existing position, the rational process requires volume and open-interest broken out on a contract-by-contract basis. Only with this data, along with price behavior and the mix of holders, can the trader hope to make a sensible evaluation.

There is an axiom about information in the market that declares: "Whenever a given piece of information is held by everyone, it has ceased to be of value to anyone." Stated another way, the market isn't going to pay you for being able to read a newspaper. Everyone can read a newspaper! Hence, reading a newspaper—although much to be recommended on general terms—won't confer much of an advantage on one.

A market bromide that works more often than not is: Buy the rumor: sell the news! By the time you can read about it in the paper, the market has likely already heard it—and has discounted it. If you're looking for a trading advantage, and everyone is, you'll have to find it in information that is not generally understood and applied. Price data is too available to confer an advantage on one who has it. Volume, open-interest, and trade-mix gives you an edge.

It is precisely for this reason that the market-technician who will devote the energy required to do his homework is sure to have a big advantage over the individual who counts on luck for his success. Maintaining a four-dimensional view of the contracts you trade in will require time and effort. No one can do this for you.

There is no service that, for a subscription fee, will assure your success in speculation. If such a service did exist, before long everybody would be a subscriber. Why not, if success were assured? And, to repeat the rule, when everyone has the information, it ceases to be of value to anyone! In view of this, be glad that profitable commodity trading does take some effort and devotion to details. Also be thankful that a lot of people who dabble in commodities are willing to take their chances on luck, hunches, and tips. These are the folks who are going to finance your speculative success!

There are a variety of sources for the price, volume, and open-interest data you require. You may want to subscribe to a charting service or a data bank (if you have the requisite computer and modem hookup). Even if you opt for one of these solutions, you will still have an important personal role in organizing and interpreting the information you get through the mail or by telephone.

Should you decide to generate your own charts, and this is certainly the preferable route if you are willing to give it the required time, all you need is a subscription to a daily newspaper that has a complete commodity section. In addition to the high-low-close that's depicted in a price-bar chart, a good commodity section will usually also show the opening-price, life-of-contract high and low, along with trade volume and adjustment up or down on open-interest in specific maturities. With a modest supply of graph paper and a straightedge, creating and maintaining your own charts becomes a brief daily task.

There is a huge benefit, however. By plotting the data on the charts for yourself, you will soon discover that you are seeing the significance of the daily entries you're making. As you watch the life of a given contract unfold a day at a time, you come to understand its personality—

and you are increasingly able to view it in perspective with other contracts in the same commodity. This is the very essence of skillful speculation!

The successful technician isn't so much analyzing and forecasting the course of prices as he or she is analyzing and forecasting the behavior of an assortment of people whose amalgam of actions will determine the course of prices. The astute technician looks behind every event that's traced out in his charts, relating it to the market participants whose interests were hurt or helped by it. Only after the trade scenario in one happening is understood, can you go on to the next development in the life of the contract under examination.

Markets behave sequentially. There is a bright or an obscure thread of continuity and cause/effect lucidity that ties each moment of market behavior to those that preceded it. It is the task of the trading technician to find this thread. Having found it, he then exerts every effort to follow it through each step of its meanderings through the life of the contract it is describing. His success in doing this job will be measured in the size of his bank accounts!

In view of the admitted and unavoidable delay in obtaining some of the technical data that the trader should ideally always have at his fingertips, some up-to-the-minute adjustments must be made in the trader's analytical methods to compensate for the lack of absolute currency of everything except price. Doing so regularly involves looking back for a few hours, a few days, or a few weeks to see what the market response has been to the stimulus of previous price movements.

The technical trader must view price as the *cause*, and changes in *volume* and *open-interest as effects*. Price is both the trigger and the yardstick by which profits and losses are measured. And profits and losses are, in turn, the only possible alternative results of speculative exposure.

With some practice and study, the chartist should be able to look back over a few weeks of price, volume, and open-interest tracings and draw some highly accurate conclusions about a contract's relative strengths and vulnerabilities. In pursuing this exercise, it's well to have a series of simple and direct questions in mind, the answers to which will provide the best available guide to whether a position should be established, increased, reduced or offset completely. Oftentimes, we must never forget, the best position is to be on the sidelines, with *no position whatever*.

Critical Technical Questions

Among the questions that the technical data should answer are these:

1. **Is the price trending up, down, or moving sideways?**

2. **Does the market show greater trading volume in connection with higher prices or lower prices?**

3. **Do open-interest changes indicate a willingness of the trade to follow higher prices or lower prices?**

4. **Is there any distinct pattern that shows open-interest and trade volume going uphill together?**

5. **Are the weak-handed, small public traders tending to overwhelmingly favor one side of the contract as compared to the other?**

6. **Are the strong-handed, large professional speculators and hedgers tending to overwhelmingly favor one side of the contract as compared to the other?**

Finding the answers to these questions will involve varying amounts of difficulty, but unless they can be resolved with some degree of finality, cautious conservatism should be your guide. You can't know what the short-term future holds in a confused technical situation, because the market is giving you no guidance. But let's assume a more technically *measurable* situation and go looking for the answers to the six questions above.

1. A *price trend* determination, if it exists, should offer no problems. A down trend characteristically presents a succession of *lower highs*, as reflected by the daily bar chart. An up trend shows a consistent tendency to *higher lows*, as reflected in the daily price bars.

2. If a spurt in volume regularly accompanies a drop in price, the chances are good that a lot of nervous longs have clustered their stop-losses close to the lower margin of the trading range. If higher price can be seen to bring a flurry of trading activity, it's the shorts who are sitting on the edge of their chairs with closely placed stops—ready to run at the first sign of trouble. If trading volume merely dries up at the upper and lower margins of a diminishing trading range, it is a fine sign that strong hands are manning the turrets on both the long and short side. If open-interest tends to hold steady or increase, while a pennant continues to take form, a major confrontation is probably shaping up. Sooner or later the trading price range must widen—when the moment of truth between the bulls and the bears will no longer be deferred. If it comes, desperation offsetting of the vanquished camp can be expected to constitute a major breakout to a higher or lower level.

3. If open-interest increases as price trends upward, the bulls are in command and full of confidence. Some shorts are being stopped out, but new sellers are taking their place. If open-interest increases as price trends lower, the bears are in command and are pressing their advantage. Some longs are offsetting, but new buyers are replacing them. In either case, the essence of a one-sided market is in the willingness of both the victors and the vanquished to follow the price. For those who are right, this means continuing to add to their profitable positions by pyramiding purchases or sales at successive price levels. For those who are wrong, it means that they must continue to absorb their losses—and constantly attract enough new victims to their cause to provide the new

selling or buying that may, at some point, be sufficient to turn the tide. When the traders begin showing reluctance to follow a price trend further, as indicated in *shrinking volume and open-interest*, a reversal is usually not far off.

4. Regardless of which direction price is trending or how far the price move has come, so long as *volume* holds up and *open-interest* remains firm or increases, the price trend is probably still intact—and should be expected to continue. Open-interest can't hold its own or grow in an up or down trend unless those unfortunates who are stopped out are quickly replaced by new buyers or sellers. Those on the winning side can usually be expected to press their advantage by pyramiding new purchases or sales—to press the trend. But unless they can find new holders to take the opposite side, a reversal *must* be anticipated. It's simply a matter of having to have losers to pay for the price-ground being covered. When the supply of losers is depleted, the party is over!

5. The weak-handed, small public traders show an overwhelming preference for the long side of any market, but this is not to say that they will *always*, and under all conditions, be long holders. There have been situations in the past when, due to strongly bearish advice from brokerage houses and other advisory sources, significant numbers of the small public trading contingent have taken the short side of a selected contract or commodity. It will happen again.

6. When the "Commitments Report" shows the large speculators and commercial hedgers to be overwhelmingly on the long or the short side of a commodity or a contract, think long and hard before placing yourself in opposition to them. It stands to reason that where the strong hands appear in near agreement as to the right side to be on, there just *must* be some sound reasons to support their sophisticated judgments.

Beware Joining the Public

The best available guide to where the public trader stands is (in the case of regulated commodities) the "Commitments of Traders" report issued by the Commodity Futures Trading Commission. As noted elsewhere, this report is available monthly and is a recapitulation of positions open at the end of the month being reported. A preparation and mailing delay of some two weeks in making it available to the trade reduces its usefulness to some degree. But it still pays to carefully review the report data, along with price action, changes in open-interest, and trading volume over the period covered in the report. By doing so, a quite reliable notion can usually be developed regarding any significant changes in posture that may have occurred in the interim between compilation of the All Positions Report and your receipt of it. Also, it offers valuable insights to the psychology of the traders, especially the big traders and hedgers.

Whenever it appears that the small public traders are heavily positioned—either long or short—in any contract, be exceedingly cautious in joining their ranks. Contrary to the oft-repeated axiom, the public is not *always* wrong; they are only wrong *most of the time*, and they may be *right* in any given trade posture. But they are always weak-handed holders, and this basic vulnerability tends to get them into trouble with great regularity.

If you feel you must join the side of the small public traders, be prepared to put your protective stops *farther away* from the discernible trading range. Sharp, short-lived flurries of stop buying and stop selling on the part of your weak-handed companions will also stop you out repeatedly, unless you anticipate their shortcomings and contrive to stay out of their line of flight in the face of small adversities.

Look for the Strong Side

Conversely, seek opportunities to join the cause of the large speculators and commercial hedgers. If trouble comes to this camp, you have allies who have both the nerves and the finances to protect their own interests—and yours—by *defensive* selling or buying. This is not to imply that such a combination can, over a period of time, keep price from moving in the direction that fundamental considerations beckon, but you can expect that it will take more than a small tactical assault to drive these strong-holders from a market position that they consider to be basically sound. In such a situation, they will defend their position, often quite tenaciously, before they will abandon it.

Check Premiums and Discounts

Often the underlying basis for such a strong-handed meeting of minds will be found in the situation as concerns *premiums* and *discounts*. Both large speculators and commercial hedgers are inclined to rely heavily on price differentials—as between cash and futures, between commodities, and between different maturities in the same commodity—in evaluating market positions.

Sell Premiums / Buy Discounts

The theory of *spreading* and *hedging* has already been treated in some detail in *Speculation in Commodity Contracts and Options*, and will not be textually repeated here. However, it will pay the trader to remember that in "normal markets," both spreaders and hedgers tend to be *buyers of discounts* and *sellers of premiums*. By seeking to follow the same general trading rationale, you can usually depend on a good deal of strong-handed assistance in protecting your position against adversity, and welcome aid in moving price to your advantage.

As will be seen later, as we delve into specific market situations for the purpose of further developing wider analytical insights, these six points are by no means the full roster of questions that might need to be answered before taking a particular market action. However, they do constitute a sound and useful preliminary procedure.

There can be no doubt that if a trader will restrict his market exposures to those situations in which *most* or, ideally, *all* of the above six points can be found favorable, he will avoid untold disappointments—and markedly improve his profits in trade.

Impetuosity is the constant enemy of most commodity speculators. They persist in taking positions on the basis of tips and hunches. Or they seize on a single attractive element—usually price movement—and pin all of their hopes on the single, unconfirmed indicator. No meteorologist would even attempt to forecast weather with nothing to assist him but a thermometer. But legions of self-described "chart traders" hopefully pursue the arcane exercise of attempting to interpret past price patterns and, from them, extrapolate the course of future price movement.

If price were the only tool available for the analytical task, then we would have to do the best job possible with this single market dimension. But we have other, and better, measurements to guide us. More particularly, we have the means of estimating not only the probabilities of price movement in a given direction, but by considering open-interest, trading volume, and the mix of position holdings, *along with* price behavior, we can develop a kind of mathematical model of the market situation in which we trade.

It's a Fast Market

Most importantly, commodity markets are highly dynamic affairs. Even if price patterns taken by themselves were as reliable as some folks want to believe, there is rarely an opportunity for the well-defined double-top, double-bottom, head-and-shoulders, or other complex chart configuration to trace itself out. The entire life of a commodity futures contract is usually limited to a matter of months. There is simply not sufficient time in which to permit a commodity price to duplicate the extensive and involved meanderings we see in securities prices.

But for even the most devout price chartist, a treasure trove of additional information awaits in the form of other data that is his or hers for the using. In combination, the four components that measure market and trader responses can take much of the peril out of speculation.

To ignore these additional market benchmarks is at once both needless and foolhardy. The techniques for applying them should not unduly tax the capabilities of any serious trader. And, to whatever extent doing so may require the trader's becoming familiar with some new concepts, the results should prove to be much more than ample reward for the effort expended in study.

4

Understanding Your Market Competition

A well-tried axiom is, "The showing you make depends on the competition." This is as true in speculation as it is in any other area of competitive activity.

Since markets do not manufacture money, but merely *transfer* money (or values) from the pockets of the losers to the pockets of the winners, it should be abundantly clear that for every market *profit* there must be a market *loss*. In fact, the sum total of the profits transferred to traders holding right positions will be somewhat *less* than the total of the losses sustained by the traders holding wrong positions. The reason for this is that a broker is nearly always involved in market transactions, and brokers collect established fees for handling the purchase and sale, or sale and purchase, of each commodity contract.

The broker's fee must be paid without respect to whether the position undertaken produces a profit or a *loss*. It is therefore apparent that *trading losses* are increased by the amount of brokers' commissions; *trading profits* are decreased by the amount of the brokerage commissions involved.

Small Public Traders

Small public traders are accorded top billing in the cast of characters that makes up the commodity market, because they are so numerous and their performance is so highly predictable.

Heading the list of the small public trader's market behaviorisms must be his insistence on occupying a *long* position. The small public trader will only rarely, if ever, sell a commodity contract short. When the public feels that prices are headed lower, they merely stand aside, waiting until they think they have an opportunity to pick bottom and establish a long position that will permit them to profit from *rising prices*.

This penchant for always being long the market is impossible to explain in terms of either economic theory or price behavior. Commodity prices, like other prices, tend to fluctuate around a median point. Both theory itself and a cursory examination of a price chart will prove to anyone's satisfaction that prices cover as much ground in down trends as they do in up trends. Moreover, commodity prices usually *fall more rapidly* than they rise, and as a consequence, the short-seller usually realizes his profits in a given position in a shorter period of time than the long in an opposite situation.

But the small public trader is not much moved by either theory or pragmatic experience. He is psychologically and irretrievably set up to be bull. You can nearly always count on his being long if he is in the market at all. And if he cannot be long, he will probably be on the sidelines.

The next most notable characteristic of the small public trader is his *impatience with a winning position* and his *tenacity when things are going against him*. The small public trader usually approaches his speculative activity with a minimum of information and exceedingly limited capital. To sustain himself in this situation, he thinks he *can only afford to make a profit*. He never even considers the possibility of taking a loss. As a result, he usually trades with badly placed stop-losses, if, indeed, he enters stop-losses at all. When prices move to his advantage, he is much more likely to take his small profits and run, instead of adding to the winning position and increasing his leverage and profit opportunities accordingly. He often runs prematurely enough to deprive himself of part or most of the benefits of the price move that is adding to his equity.

Too Much Bravery Can Break You

In the reverse situation though, the public trader is a paragon of persistence and self-control. He will watch prices move against him day after day, rather than sell the position out for a modest loss and move to the sidelines until another opportunity presents itself. He sticks by his guns and sees a small loss grow into a debacle. When he does close out his losing position, he is most likely to do so at or near the bottom of the move or at the end of his financial resources.

To sum up these facets of small trader personality: He does not have the self-control or the market discipline required to take a *small loss*. Neither does he have the courage and fortitude to stay with a winning position and pyramid toward a maximum return on the price move.

Finally, small public traders, like sheep, tend to come and go in bunches. When a particular commodity begins to catch the small public trader's fancy, the word can be expected to travel rapidly. As the throng of new public position holders grows, prices will climb upward since, as previously noted, this classification of trader is usually only interested in *buying*. And their sheer force of numbers, coupled with a general lack of market awareness, regularly leads them into paying up for the contracts they want to acquire.

The higher prices climb, the more attractive the opportunity looks to other public traders who have remained on the sidelines, waiting to see if a real move is under way. More and more of them join the flock. At some point, however, the reservoir of new public traders is certain to be depleted, with the result that there is insufficient new buying to keep pushing prices progressively higher. It can be taken as gospel that a market that can't go up will go down. When the reversal comes at the end of a bull-trend blowoff, the latest arrivals on the long side will be immediately confronted by losses as prices move lower. Their selling will begin as a trickle, grow into a stream, and end up as a flood.

Before the last of the small public traders have departed a deteriorating situation, the earliest purchasers will have taken some profits. Another segment of the public trader group will have approximately broken even, and the remainder will have suffered losses—some of them impressive losses.

It may appear Machiavellian to detail this sequence of events and label it as a predictable phenomenon in market behavior for a large group of participants. However, the evidence is too clear to be rebutted on any basis whatsoever. And it is precisely for this reason that when any market professional refers to "weak hands" you can be sure that he is talking about small public traders. Lack of *information*, lack of *capital*, and lack of a firm *trading program* can be counted on to get them in trouble. Additionally, the weak hands of the public are likely to cause a good deal of trouble for other more astute and more cautious speculators, who just happen to be associated with them on what turns out to be the wrong side of the market. Experienced traders have difficulty sleeping soundly when they know that they have large numbers of small traders keeping them company in a substantial commodity position.

Large Speculators

The two things that distinguish this group of traders are market experience and financial ability. And such qualifications are not happy accidents. Their experience has come from long exposure in the market, and their adequate financing has been generated by successful application of a more or less consistently applied speculative program. The large public speculator may be a full-time trader with no other business. Or he may be an individual who divides his time between trading activities and another business or profession. In any case, the large public speculator has learned his lessons and has taken them to heart. He knows how to accept a small loss and forget it. More important, he knows how to pyramid paper profits into ever larger holdings, with the result that he always tends to maximize his profit opportunities and minimize his losses. This produces a situation in which an individual can be confident that if he is right even 45 percent of the time, he stands to make money. The reason is simply that the profits he realizes from his right positions are substantially larger than the losses he experiences on his wrong positions.

The large public speculator is usually a "Lonesome George" kind of operator. He does his own market homework—very carefully—and weighs profit opportunities against loss risk with meticulous care before establishing a new position. He would just as soon be short as long, and he will nearly always know precisely how much impairment he will accept before stepping aside. Likewise, every position will have an identifiable profit objective. Before undertaking any new position, the large trader will likely have a stop-loss point directly in mind, along with a point at which the second story will be put on the position pyramid.

This large trader will not be stampeded into deserting a good position for small reasons. Neither will he pay up to establish a new long position nor sell down for the purpose of establishing a new short position. He ordinarily has a rather firm notion about the level at which he is willing to buy or sell, and unless the market will fill his orders in the acceptable range, he has the patience to wait.

It should not be surprising to learn that the large speculator represents "strong hands" in the marketplace. He reflects the qualities of judgment, experience, and adequate capitalization, which enable him to take a major role in the market function. His trading prowess is attested to by his financial success, and his market wisdom is an important factor in upgrading the qualitative performance of futures markets in their essential function of price discovery and price forecasting.

Hedgers—Commercial Interests

In a market seminar several years ago, a professional speculator was asked how he would describe his market activities. With only the briefest hesitation, Bernard P. Carey replied, "I try to figure out what the hedgers are going to do; then I do it *first!*"

It would be a serious mistake to consider the answer even slightly facetious.

If you can figure out what the hedgers are going to do and then do it first, Croesus would envy your bank account in due course. There are several reasons why *being with the hedgers* (or, even better, preceding them) makes excellent trading sense: First, bonafide hedgers are *not limited by law*—as speculators are—in the amounts they can buy, sell, or hold in open positions in the futures markets. Second, they are extremely strong hands—with the business requirements and finances to buy or sell in multiples of millions of pounds or bushels whenever the situation looks promising. Third, with huge positions held open in the market, hedgers have the proprietary interest required to prompt *defensive* buying or selling when price change appears to threaten their interests.

Finally, hedgers must be accepted as among the best market analysts to be found. Continuous exposure to it, and constant involvement in it, can be expected to make some kind of an authority out of anyone with sufficient intelligence to learn and heed the lessons experience necessarily brings. Hedgers can *teach* the serious speculator much, or *cost* him much, depending on whether the trader tries to understand and emulate their practices or whether he merely sees them as a passive element in the market and ignores them.

"If you can't lick 'em, join 'em," is a sensible admonition in several areas of human involvement. It is particularly appropriate in the market. The speculators in the market are far more numerous than the hedgers, but their holdings usually fall far short of the open commitments in the hands of so-called commercial interests. And the hedgers' potentials for trading into an attractive situation are, as stated previously, unhampered by most of the strictures that the CFTC and individual exchanges impose on speculators.

Understand the Hedgers' Approach

Taken all together, speculative traders will only rarely be able to match the hedgers' market muscle. So, it always pays to respect the hedgers, even though you don't choose to join them. It is too much to expect that mere alignment with the majority of commercial interests will *always* result in profits, but it is completely safe to say that by traveling with such a crowd, the probabilities of realizing a profit on a selected market position—or on the average of all such positions—is very much enhanced.

By developing the capability of looking at the market through the hedgers' eyes, the speculator will discover an entirely new dimension in price. He will learn to recognize a given price as *cheap or dear,* as it compares to *other prices.* Such an appraisal is invariably going to be more useful in planning market actions than any empirical notion about whether a solitary price is too high or too low, per se.

It takes great flexibility to maintain an open mind on the matter of price. However, the best traders are those who have no firm idea about the right price of anything, except as a relative measurement. More on this later.

A clear line of distinction is usually drawn between speculators and hedgers, and perhaps undeservedly. While, by definition, a speculator is a buyer and seller of the risks of ownership, as measured in price change, a hedger—again by definition—is someone who seeks to avoid the very risk exposures that the speculator welcomes. Still, the *hedger seeks profits* in the market, just as the speculator does. The most important consideration is the differing manners in which speculators and hedgers pursue their profit objectives within the market framework.

The hedging function has been treated in adequate detail elsewhere, so their doings will not be extensively explained here. Suffice it to say that a hedger—or commercial interest—attempts to minimize his opportunities for loss on a cash inventory (or obligation) by selling (or buying) an equal amount of futures contracts in the market. Since cash prices and futures prices tend to move up and down together, hedge protection is obtained by simultaneously holding a cash inventory long and a futures position short—or vice versa.

Profit Lures All Market Users

To summarize this discussion, competition is the very soul of the marketplace. There need never be the slightest doubt about the objective of *anyone* who takes part in its activity: profit, in one form or another, is the only possible reason. Trading methods of the hedgers and the speculators differ, but this is due to the differing natures of their overall business requirements. Everyone is attempting to buy at low prices and sell at higher prices.

The greatest distinctions to be found among the several categories of the trade have to do with relative strengths in situations that invite aggressive exploitation—or responses in the face of reversals. It has often been said, "Scared money never wins anything." You can believe it. The anxieties that always accompany over-trading not only destroy the decision-making ability, but trading beyond one's financial ability to take possible losses opens the door to irretrievable financial ruin. Fear, in such a situation, must be a constant companion.

Speculative success is a practice in patience, caution, and Spartan courage when opportunity beckons. The market is the only authority on price, and traders who forget this fact pay dearly for their lapses.

Traders Often Overbuy and Oversell

The thing that makes technical trading lucrative is that *traders* regularly succeed in *distorting prices* above or below the right level, as gauged by balances between supply and demand. Such a condition cannot exist for long, however, due to the sheer size and strength of the total markets involved. Anytime an overbought or oversold situation develops, the abberration reflects collective error on the part of a particular group of traders. When the technical correction occurs, it is the result of irresistible market realities asserting themselves—and returning price to whatever level is justified by the facts inherent in the current market.

The skillful technical trader is able to recognize price distortions when they occur, and trade *against* them. In so doing, he helps contain them and, while adding to his own trading profits, upgrades the quality of the composite pricing function that takes place in the pits.

It is an altogether valid, valuable, and profitable trading practice and one that enhances market efficiency at the same time it adds to the technician's bank account.

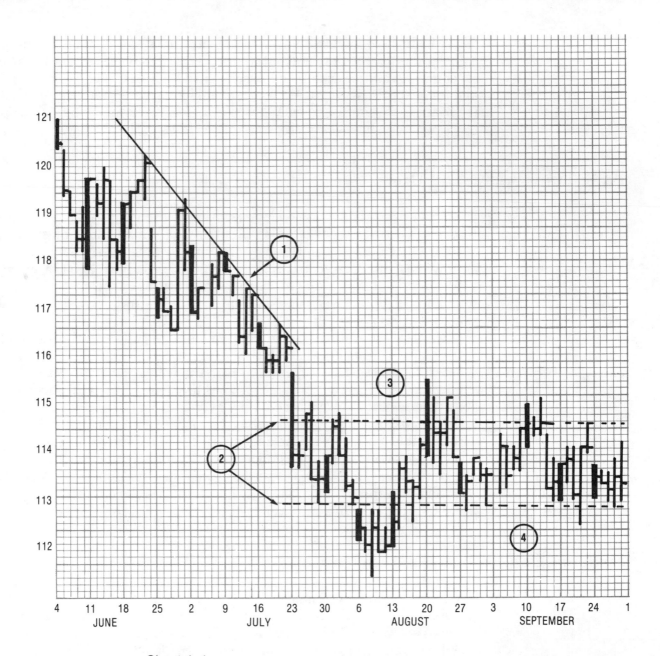

Chart 4–1

This chart reflects several well-known market behaviorisms:

(1) is a clear-cut *down trend*, reflecting a major market reevaluation of the proper price/value level as dictated by fundamentals. (2) identifies the new trading range. (3) marks the high-price area that is reached as a result of short-squeezes or "over-buying." (4) is the low-priced area that represents the results of long-squeezes or "over-selling."

By *buying dips* and *selling bulges*, technically inclined speculators help keep price fluctuations within some variable range that constitutes the market's current *price-idea*.

5

How to Think
about the Major
Market Indicators

As the following chapters dealing with price, volume, and open-interest will indicate, each of these considerations serve to shed some degree of useful light on trader actions and reactions. Of the three indicators, price has the most impressive following. Indeed, there are some chartists who insist that by analyzing *past* patterns traced out on a simple bar chart, showing only daily (or weekly) trading ranges and closes, they can reliably project *future* price behavior.

Other chart users are willing to put almost unquestioning faith in point-and-figure plottings—buying, selling, or holding in accordance with the patterns that arise from this technique.

The author has, in company with several other well-experienced market investigators, devoted a good bit of both time and effort to analytical price charting. The methodology pursued has involved all of the standard charting procedures, both bar and point-and-figure. A separate plotting of moving averages was employed in some forecasting models, using several different time segments. In yet another exercise, combinations of both futures and cash commodity prices were fed into a computer, variously weighted and taken off as composites, in an effort to produce an *assembled market value* that might be useful in forecasting price direction.

Individual Trader Needs Differ

For whatever reasons, results proved indeterminate. Price data alone failed to produce the qualitative results required to profitably base mar-

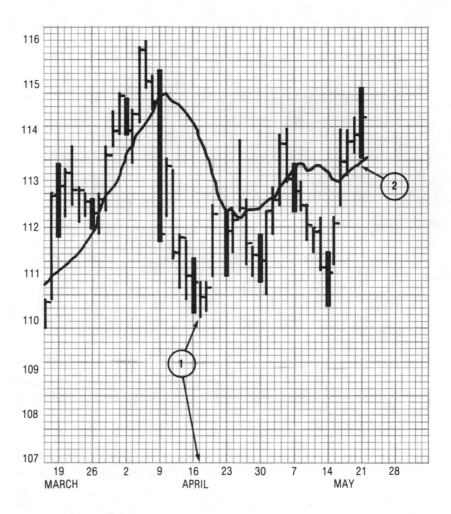

Chart 5-1

Use of a moving-average plotting can be of some value in trading markets that follow long-term trends with a minimum of technical fireworks. However, in contracts like the one above, if the trader follows the usual practice of buying on each ascending crossover and selling on each downside violation of the average, he is likely to have put himself squarely into the whipsaw.

Until April 17 (1), this 10-day moving average worked well (provided one ignores less than ½-cent penetrations).

From April 25 through the balance of the charted period, the average (2) is, at best, fickle leadership. If the time period of the average is increased to 20 or 30 days, its usefulness (in this situation) is even worse.

---

ket decisions on them. This is not intended to imply that price-only charting procedures are useless. Each trader must answer this question for himself, and the answer will be found in his profit-and-loss records. Anything that improves speculative profitability should be used, including things that do not seem to work equally well for others. Each market participant brings his own unique mix of information and discernment to bear on the problems of trading. There may be those who

---

Price Movement Significance

In a positive sense, price pattern tells you whether the bulls or the bears are in clear-cut control of the situation or if the opposing forces are stalemated in a trading range in which neither side seems able to demonstrate definitive superiority in moving price to their advantage.

In a negative sense, price movement tells you who is in trouble. And while fundamental considerations and trade psychology will move a market, trouble will move it even faster!

Trade Volume Significance

In a positive sense, trade volume provides a measurement of the enthusiasm or urgency the trade feels to do something at the given price level. Since the majority of all trader decisions have some reference to price, increasing volume must be viewed as a reflection of increasing opportunities traders on both sides see in the contract—for whatever reason—at the existing price level.

Negatively, trade volume measures the urgency with which those who are in trouble view their situation. Within a relatively restricted trading range, both the bulls and the bears may be content to merely wait, rather than either running for cover through offset or pressing their respective sides of the market. In such a standoff, volume may be minimal. However, let price move definitively higher *or* lower, and volume will tell you how anxious the disadvantaged traders are to get out—and how eager the new, or existing speculators on the winning side, are to take initial positions or enlarge current holdings at the revised price level.

---

need nothing more than a visual reference of past price behavior and their own evaluative abilities to arrive at the right decisions in the market. For your author, however, price data is not sufficient by itself. Or, to put it another way, by combining the information contained in *volume* and *open-interest* with *price data,* vastly better trading decisions are made.

The reason that several indicators serve the trader better than any single one should become obvious as the contents of this book are digested.

Like the doctor's chart that shows the temperature, pulse, and respiration of his patient, the serious trader in commodities should at least have ready access to a chart reflecting price, trading volume, and open-interest. The added facets of information will certainly improve his continuing perspective of the market in which he is dealing.

In order to put these three market indicators into useful focus, it pays to develop both a positive and a negative appraisal for each of them.

Combined Indicators Give Clearer View

By combining these individual considerations, we can arrive at a two-dimensional, or even a three-dimensional, view of the technical market

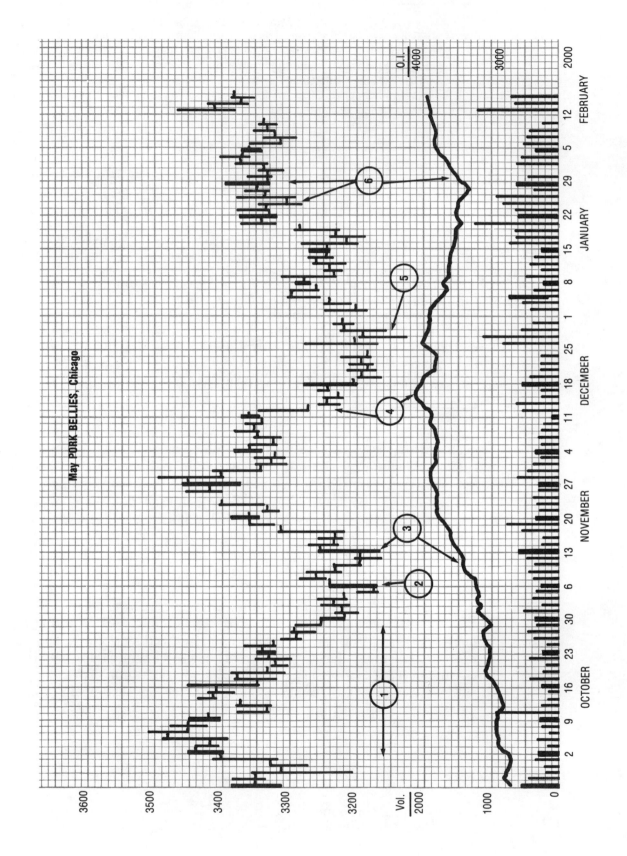

Chart 5-2

This pork belly contract shows how trade sentiment can change from bullish to bearish in a very short time and how volume and open-interest will tell you it's happening.

During all of October (1), the trade followed price lower with real enthusiasm—as measured in open contracts. The twin lows (2) of November 3 and 6 chased out some holders, but without any hint of a panic—as witness the small volume. Open-interest picked up on the brief bulge but flattened out (3) on the interim-low of the 10th. From November 13 to the 27th, both trade volume and open-interest tended to spurt on higher prices and to shrink on setbacks.

Failure to make a new high on the 28th markedly tempered the conflict about price direction, and after a few weak shorts were chased out, price sagged, paused, then fell more. Difference of opinion began to grow (4) around the 3250 level but flagged once more under 3200. The whipsaw (5) caught the shorts on the 26th and grabbed the bulls the very next day.

Now we note that throughout January the trade is reluctant to increase its holdings and follow price higher. It's only after the weak longs have been squeezed out (6) on January 24, 25, and edgy shorts on 29, that some real technical strength appears to support a move to higher levels.

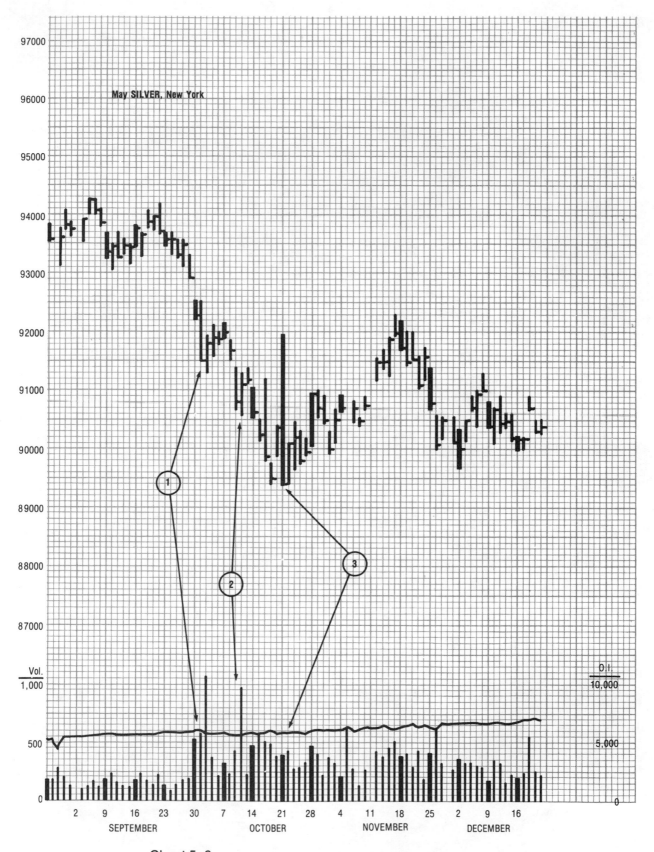

Chart 5-3

In contrast to the highly responsive open-interest index in the preceding chart, the volume of holdings in May silver offered little useful guidance for the technical trader.

Lower prices elicited no significant change in the inclinations of traders to increase or reduce their open positions. The same was true of higher prices. *(cont. on next page)*

Chart 5-3 *(concluded)*

Except for a modest two-day whipsaw (1) on October 1 and 2, and a bad scare for the shorts (2) in a very tight trading range on October 10, the 4,000-point decline in this contract was an extremely orderly affair.

October 21 was a most interesting session. Note (3) how eagerly some weak shorts wanted out but how reluctantly the bulls accommodated them. This is a classical demonstration of what can happen when a collection of "resting" stop-loss orders get touched off in a relatively modest fluctuation. Once touched, the squeeze is not likely to be halted until everything "resting" is filled. And if the other side doesn't feel like accommodating the losers, the situation can turn into an impressive price move—although a short-lived one.

Open-Interest Significance

In a positive sense, open-interest is a *quantitative* indication of the level of attractiveness the contract offers to all classes of potential market participants. With some 40 commodities traded on north American exchanges, there is a good deal of competition for speculative attention. Moreover, events related to nature, politics, and economic relationships may put a given commodity in the limelight for a period of time—and just as suddenly drop it from speculative favor. Market liquidity must always be a matter of primary concern for the speculator, and there is no better barometer of liquidity than the open-interest figure.

In a negative sense, open-interest provides excellent clues to what the losers are doing about their problem. Open-interest will also tell you if the positions being abandoned by the offsetting losers are being taken up by others, since it continually lets you know if total participation in the contract is shrinking, expanding, or merely holding its own. Significant changes in open-interest must be carefully analyzed, unless the trader is prepared to deal with some terrible surprises.

---

condition. Armed with this kind of appraisal, the trader can develop some keen and highly useful insights into the nature of a development that has recently taken place—or may be in process. From this point of departure, he can go on to forecast the probable next phase of trader response or reaction.

To assist the reader in developing his ability in recognizing the obvious technical signals and also help him translate various *indicator combinations* into a useful *action/reaction* rationale, some essential technical rules now follow. Along with each rule is a chart presentation of the principles involved, and a brief explanation of the events which give rise to the first effect and create the requisite technical strength or weakness that makes a specific *reaction* probable.

All examples demonstrate characteristic situations, and while there is—and can be—no such thing as a sure-fire trading formula, by applying these rationalities to actual trading problems, even the most inexperienced technical trader will be struck by how often the same charades play themselves out in the futures markets. The principal hazard is essentially always the same: putting too much reliance on *any single concept* in trade activities. Technical considerations can, in a particular situation, outweigh even the most powerful fundamental considerations. In another kind of market make-up, the steam may be taken out of a potentially explosive technical buildup by what is deemed to be only a mi-

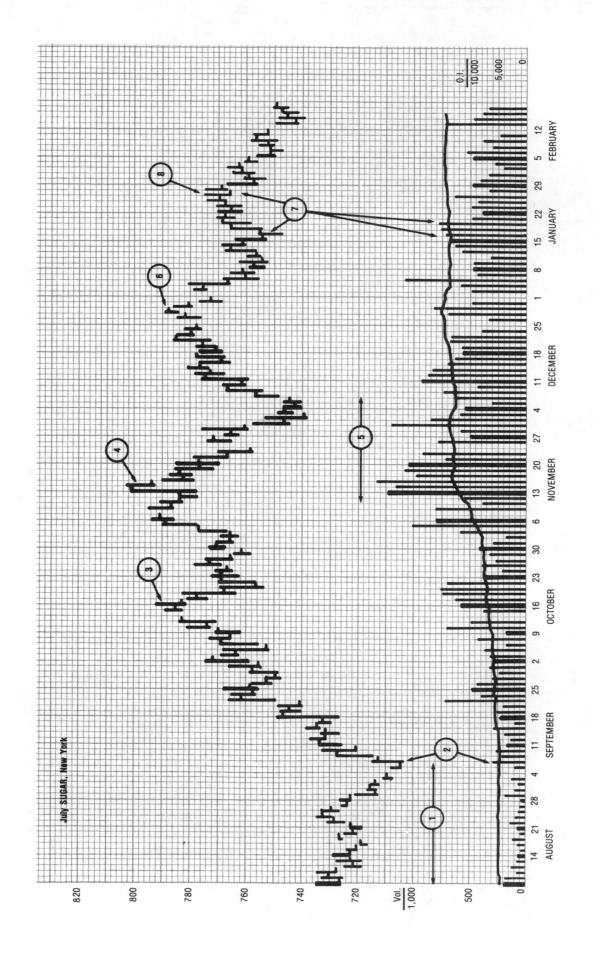

July SUGAR, New York

Chart 5-4

It would be a simple thing to make a fortune in commodity speculation if every contract turned in the stellar performance of July sugar, shown on the above chart.

(1) For the first month of the contract, the trade just refused to do business at any reduction in price. Although open-interest stayed level, volume shrunk to nothing on price dips. Then (2) on September 6, a clear reversal took place, with the jump in volume to confirm it.

Throughout September and up to October 16, price, volume, and open-interest all bore the distinctive mark of the confident bulls. A second reversal took place on October 16 (3)—again with good volume to qualify it. The next four sessions took out a lot of weak longs, and some weak shorts on the 20th's sharp upside reversal. We next see volume and open-interest both expanding, as prices move toward the new contract high—and the key reversal (4) on November 14.

The trade didn't follow the three-week sell-off (5) with much enthusiasm, as evidenced in open-interest. But by December 27 (6), the bears were in command, and, except for a minor technical reaction in late January (7), lower prices were the rule.

It is clear that failure to make a new interim high on January 26 (8), was a major disappointment to the bullish contingent.

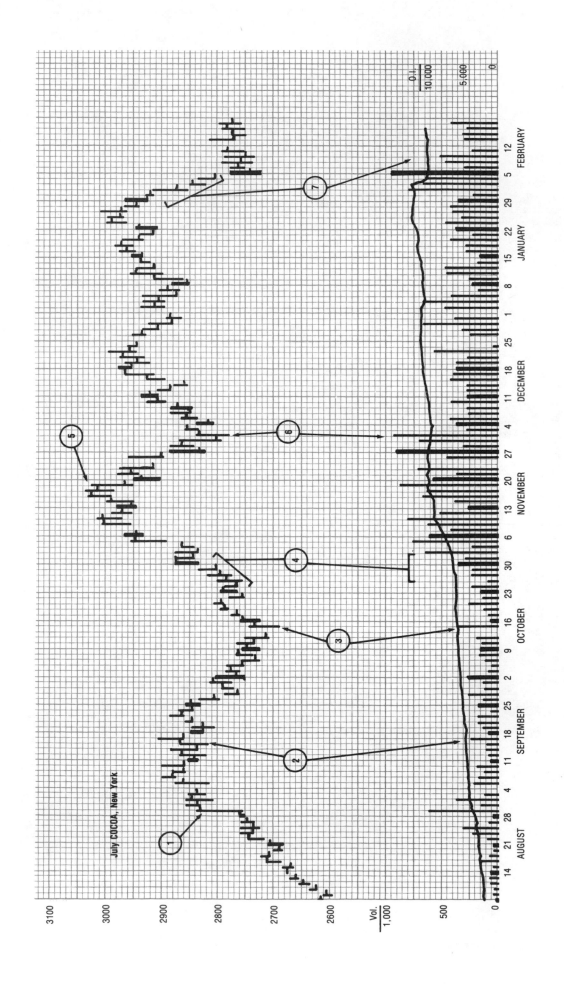

Chart 5-5

The bulls took hold of this July cocoa with a firm grip from the start, but there was no lack of needed opposition to take the short side. Even the rather substantial short-squeeze on September 1 was fully maintained in prices the following day (1). Hindsight would identify market actions on September 15 (2) and October 13 (3) as key reversals—but the price/volume symptoms were not particularly convincing at the time.

It wasn't until October 30 that the technicians really got a signal. Four successively higher markets on moderate volume, followed by a gap and accompanied by good open-interest increments (4), spelled higher prices. From this point, it was almost straight up for 150 points.

Action on November 16 (5) was unclear, but the next day's 75-point range and a close almost on the bottom—along with record volume—was convincing evidence of a turn-around.

Dropping open-interest and low volume on the 28th and 29th had alerted the shorts that the trade wasn't following the sell-off, so the interim-low on high volume—and the high-er close—on the 30th (6) was no surprise. Prices were headed higher once more.

Finally, note the sharp drop in price, volume, and open-interest in early February (7). Traders who saw this as a technical signal of vast proportions took part in a cocoa bull move of more than 2,000 points over the following 10 months!

nor revision in information available concerning supply/demand equilibrium.

The key to profitable commodity speculation is to be aware of all the elements that can bear importantly on the course of prices. This includes fundamentals, of course, and it also includes trader psychology and reactionary behavior under the twin goads of avarice and fear. While it is true that we may never be sure what the market will do under a given stimulus, we do know a good deal about how traders react in the face of beckoning opportunity or mounting losses. The fascinating activity of pursuing speculation on the basis of what we expect the traders to do next is the essence of technical market analysis.

There are a good many predictables that can be set forth to guide our first exploratory footsteps, some of which are indicated in the following charts.

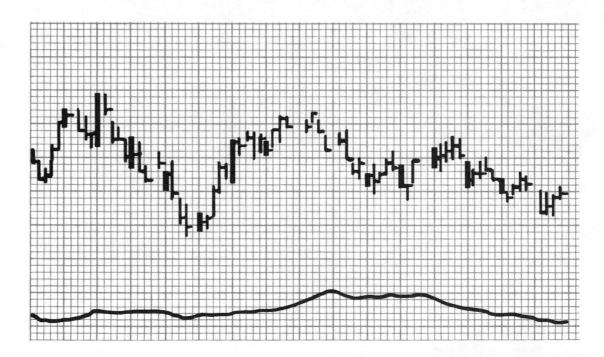

Chart 5-6

Since a long and a short are required for each commodity contract held open, it is perfectly clear that any time open-interest increases, there is both new buying and new selling. The new buying deserves the main emphasis, however, since the buyers are succeeding in moving prices to their advantage.

In the face of any price rise, we must assume that a certain amount of loss-induced offsetting on the part of disadvantaged shorts is taking place. In order for open-interest to be maintained, new shorts must step forward to take the place of those who depart. Whenever replacements for the offsetting losers do not appear, the upside move must come to an end.

However, as long as open-interest is increasing, the bull move can be considered to have the required financing to draw on. The longs can be expected to press their advantage and fight to hold the market initiative.

Rule: When open-interest goes up and price goes up, bulls are in command. New buying is present.

Chart 5-7

Everything that was said in connection with the bull move under the previous rule applies here—in the opposite frame of reference.

An increase in open-interest indicates willingness on the part of the trade to enlarge commitments in the contract being examined. When open holdings increase in connection with a move to lower prices, you can assume that some impaired positions are being closed out. But the long losers that are selling out are being supplanted, either by new bulls or existing holders of long positions. If this were not the case, open-interest would drop, since it is also a certainty that some short-holders will take profits on any move to their advantage.

The situation to which this rule applies is one in which the bulls are losing but recruiting allies at an increasing rate. The bears are on the offensive and pressing the issue with increasing sales. So long as open-interest continues to swell, the trend can be expected to persist.

Rule: When open-interest goes up and price goes down, bears are in command. New selling is present.

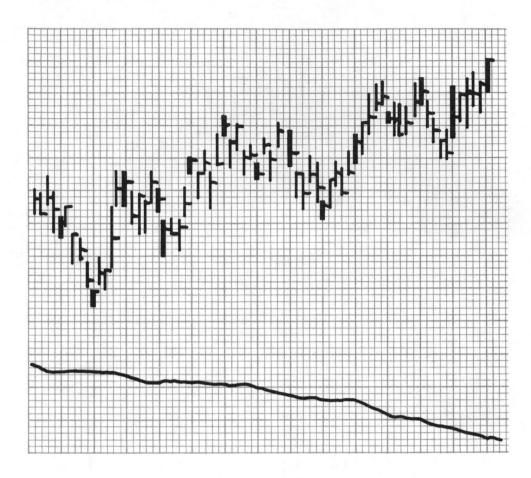

Chart 5-8

Any time higher price produces a reduction in open-interest, it is because the losers are unable to attract new holders to their cause as rapidly as the existing forces are deserting. In connection with a price rise, of course, it's the shorts who are in trouble and the longs who are riding high and stacking up profits.

The weakness that this combination of circumstances indicates stems from the fact that, once the impaired short positions have been bought in, the remaining demand from market longs is usually unequal to the task of holding prices at their "squeeze" level. When the buying pressure subsides, selling pressure will come to the fore, and then it will be the longs who are in retreat, with the shorts hot on their heels.

Rule: When open-interest goes down as price goes up, shorts are offsetting. The situation is technically weak.

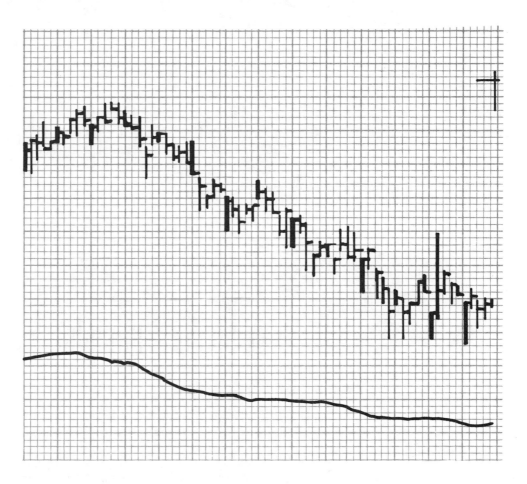

Chart 5-9

Whenever open-interest declines in the face of a price move in *either* direction, it is proof-positive that losers are offsetting and that new position holders are not appearing in sufficient numbers to take their place. Of course, in order for open-interest to shrink, *both sides* of open positions must be offset. Thus, we can conclude that in such a situation the long-losers are closing out at a loss, and the short winners are cashing paper profits.

However, long-offsetting is the main consideration here. Once the disappointed longs have given up, offerings will diminish and the stage will be set for a greater or lesser rebound to the upside. Since, by definition, a technical move represents a departure from the "right" price (as measured by supply/demand balance), once the technical imbalance is corrected, price can be expected to return to its equilibrium level.

Rule: When open-interest goes down as price goes down, longs are offsetting. The situation is technically strong.

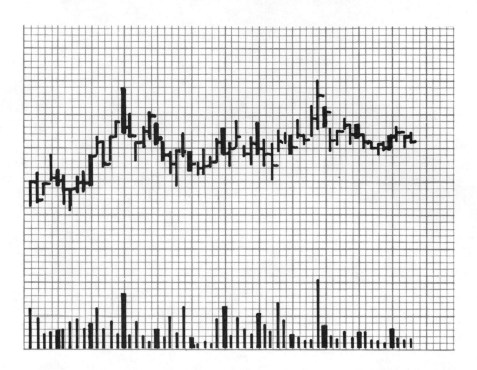

Chart 5–10

A burst of trade volume accompanied by strongly rising price should always be viewed with great suspicion. Volume is the urgency indicator—and nothing creates urgency faster than losses.

Certainly a new bit of bullish news can also create urgency on the part of those who want to take new long positions or enlarge their present holdings. But squeezed shorts are the most eager of all buyers. Even when the volume explosion involves large elements of both offsetting and new demand, caution is still called for, because it is written that whatever the traders do, they overdo!

Blindly buying a new-high price level when accompanied by inordinately high volume can put you squarely in the teeth of an overbought short-squeeze. When the reversal comes, you will be faced with immediate impairment that a little more patience and analysis can often avoid.

Solid price rises usually reflect increased volume, but it takes a crowd of hurt shorts to create the classical frenzy of an up-side "blowoff." Buying such an event can put you on the wrong side of a key reversal and cost you dearly.

Rule: When trade volume goes up and price goes up, there is new buying pressure. Either shorts are offsetting, or new demand—or both. View the situation with suspicion!

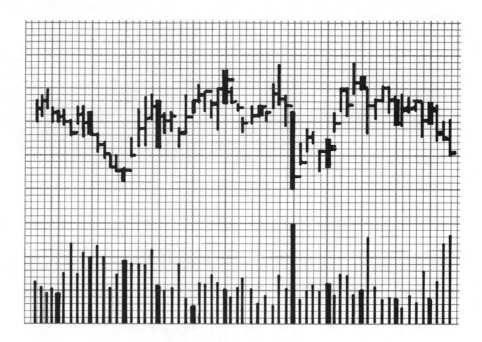

Chart 5–11

The chart shows a typical long-squeeze. Price made a new interim low on September 25. Longs had, for several months, been planting their stop-losses right below the trading range. The slide in early August took a lot of the weak-handed longs out, but good buying support contained the potential crisis. When the price went through this lower range, it spelled trouble. As volume swelled, the price dropped ever lower. Only after making a new contract low did support appear.

Characteristically, once the weak-handed longs were out of the contract, the price moved sharply higher. Events like this are not rarities. They underscore the importance of being constantly aware of the vulnerability of the contract, based purely on the likely placement of large groups of stop-loss orders.

Rule: When trade volume goes up and price goes down, there is increased selling pressure. Either longs are offsetting, or new offerings—or both. View the situation with suspicion!

Chart 5–12

Once the weak hands have been forced to buy in their short holdings in the face of a price bulge, the buying pressure *must* fall off. With the disadvantaged shorts now taken care of, the most eager buyers are now gone. All that remains is the business-as-usual demand from takers of new positions and perhaps a scattering of purchases by old longs that want to increase their holdings. Both of these categories are going to be quite choosy about the price levels at which they will do business. Unlike the running shorts, these buyers can insist on lower prices or refuse to do business.

With no traders left who are willing to reach for the contracts they want, a downside reaction is the best prospect in sight. The quiet spell following big volume and soaring price may last a few minutes or a few sessions, but, in any case, it represents a time of regrouping among the market forces. The upside move stops because the supply of losing shorts is temporarily depleted.

**Rule: When trade volume goes down and price goes up, buying pressure is drying
        up. A downside reaction is likely. Don't buy a quiet market after a rise.**

Chart 5-13

This is the obverse of the situation described in the preceding rule. If the downside move brings big volume and heavy selling on the part of brokerage houses, you can be sure that stop-losses are a major factor in the situation. This is because brokerage houses handle all of the public's orders, and public traders are almost never big short-sellers. When the public looms large on the selling side of the market, it represents offsetting—either in the face of loss or for the purpose of cashing paper profits.

Once the weak bulls have given up and sold out, the flood of orders that pressed price and made volume explode is ended. Routine selling by new and existing shorts won't be up to the task of keeping the pressure on price.

Rule: When volume goes down and price goes down, selling pressure is diminishing. An upside reaction is likely. Don't sell a quiet market after a fall.

The continuing quest of the technical trader is to find situations in which unanimity exists among the major indicators. Such occasions may be rare, but when they can be found, they usually prove to be well worth the search. Any time the three-dimensional view of the market shows agreement among the indicators, it will pay to study the situation long and hard.

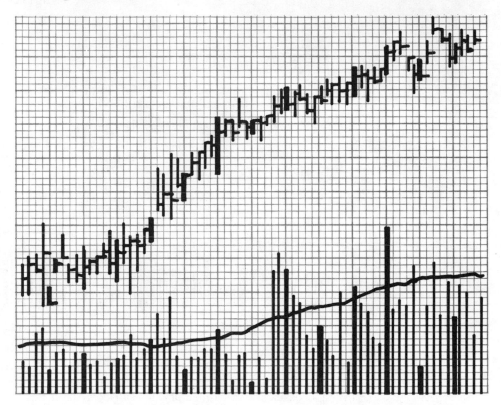

Chart 5-14

If a trader can find two or three of these situations each year, his speculative results should be most impressive. When such an opportunity arises, it deserves careful and highly aggressive exploitation.

The principal warning should be to remember that "one swallow doesn't make a spring." Major price moves usually have to spend some time building a base before the climb begins. Wait for the market to tell you that the upside move is underway. You will know it when all three indicators show clear tendencies to move together.

Be alert for *volume* and *open-interest* changes that will warn you against upcoming "tops"—and keep your stops close enough to protect your profits at *all times*. However, don't try to decide when a market like this has gone far enough. No one knows what constitutes a high price except the market. You will know that prices are high enough when the triple signal begins breaking down and the symptoms become those of a two-way trade.

Rule: When price is going up, along with increasing open-interest and increasing trade volume, the situation is extremely bullish. This triple signal often indicates a major price move to a higher value plateau.

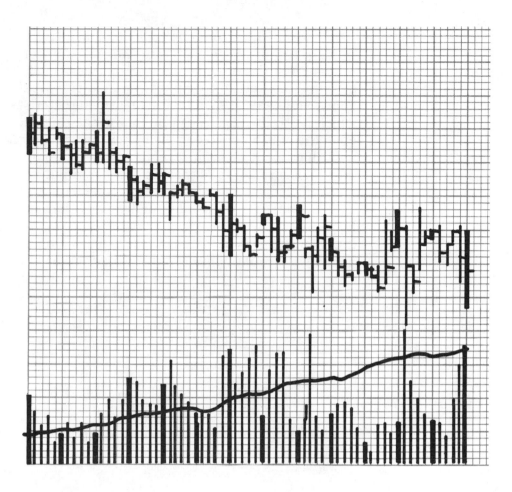

Chart 5–15

This is the combination that gladdens the hearts of the bears. When all three of the major indicators agree that prices are too high, an impressive drop is usually in store.

The thing that plagues traders most in markets of this kind is impatience. After running up excellent profits, each small reversal tempts them to take their profits and run. This, in fact, is why weak hands seldom make much money in the market. Even with everything going their way, they lack the courage and self-control to pyramid and maximize the opportunity.

Or, what's worse, they see a technical reversal as the end of the trend—they buy in their short holdings and then go long. Once the technical move is out of the way, price resumes its downward path—and the quick-change artist loses his earlier profits in the most ridiculous exercise imaginable: arguing with the market.

Don't expect perfect performance from the market. Reasonable predictability is all you can hope for, and that should be enough to insure anyone's overall success.

Rule: When price is moving lower, along with increasing open-interest and increasing trade volume, the situation is extremely bearish. This triple signal often indicates a major price move to substantially lower value level.

There are other combinations that can be fashioned from the four aspects of technical consideration and stated as more or less firm technical trading rules or guides. But the purpose of this volume is not to declare axioms but to teach the commodity speculator how to analyze, apply, and capitalize on the technical characteristics of the markets in which he trades. Rules can be forgotten! But once a trader has developed the ability to look at the major market symptoms and arrive at a valid judgment about its technical health, he has moved permanently into that elite group of market users who put every confidence in skill and knowledge—and let the others depend on guesses and hunches.

Once a trader has come to understand the basics of technical market behavior, she will never forget the concepts involved. Practice in applying them can only have the effect of sharpening their usefulness and enhancing the profitability of the speculator who knows how to use them.

6

Understanding Price as a Measurement of Values

We live with prices constantly, finding them usually too high when we're buying and, likewise, too low when we're selling. A good price for anything depends on whether we *have* some of it or *want* some of it.

All markets, of which commodity exchanges represent perhaps the most sophisticated examples, can best be viewed as arenas in which functional compromises are worked out between the seekers of high prices (sellers) and seekers of low prices (buyers). While a commodity exchange also attracts supplies (assembles), standardizes quality (grades), and distributes (transfers ownership), the basic activity taking place on a future exchange is price discovery. Buyers and sellers meet through their respective brokers in the pits and hammer out their individual trades through the machinery of an open-outcry auction.

Since vital commodities have always represented merchandise in relative shortage, it is difficult to ever foresee a day when grain, meat, or silver would be without some value—or some degree of salability. At the other end of the spectrum, we know that world-shattering shortages can occur in which case prices can only be limited by the extent of human desire to keep eating and living, and the ability to pay the price required.

Thus we can hypothesize the lowest price at something near a zero economic return—or an actual loss—to those who produced it and transported it to market. The highest price imaginable is virtually without limit, depending on the need someone feels for the merchandise, and his ability and willingness to pay up to get it. Since we know that markets discover prices in the trade between buyers and sellers, we might ask

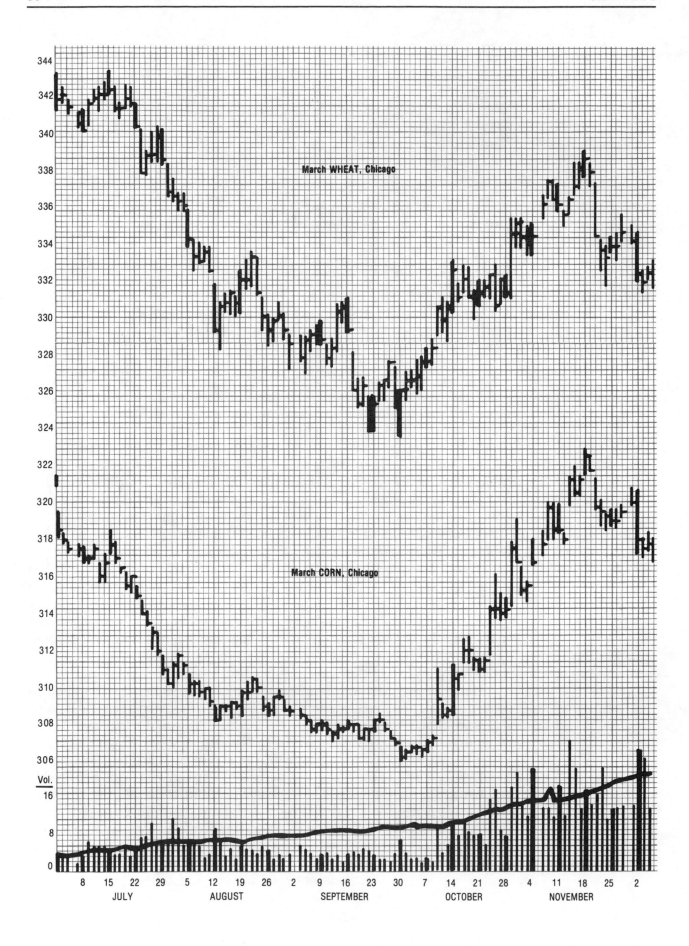

March WHEAT, Chicago

March CORN, Chicago

Chart 6-1

The trader who confines his appraisal of price to the myopic view of what "looks" high or low deprives himself of the vastly more reliable guidance that can be found in price comparisons.

In terms of major use applications, wheat and corn might appear to be poor substitutes for each other. Wheat is essentially a human food, and corn is largely consumed by animals. In spite of this, the two grains maintain relative pricing that tends to be extremely consistent.

Any number of substitutive combinations can be found in the commodity complex, reflecting various degrees of price/value interaction. In addition to comparisons between commodities (or various contracts in the same commodity), price spreads between market locations can also be highly enlightening.

Price is a fickle, highly relative consideration. Before deciding that *any* price level is wrong, check it against some of the other available yardsticks. Traders have a history of being wrong at least as often as market-assigned values are.

---

why it is that wheat is currently selling for about $3.50 per bushel. Why not $2.30, or $6.50—or 30 cents?

Substitutability Makes Prices

The obvious answer is that there are people who are willing to sell wheat at $3.50 per bushel; therefore, no one needs to pay more. The surface fact in most food categories is that the seller (producer) usually appears to have a demonstrable advantage in price determination. He does not have to sell his output to live (at least in theory), but the nonproducer (buyer) must acquire food or starve. In practice, however, this oversimplification breaks down quickly. The buyer does not have to buy wheat to stay alive. He can make bread out of rye, corn, or soybean meal. Or he can eat meat, fish, or vegetables. Moreover, within reason, he will buy alternative foods if wheat prices get too high. As a consequence, the permissible range of wheat prices is not the full reach from zero to the infinite capability of an affluent, hungry man. The most meaningful limitation on the price of wheat—or anything else—is oftentimes its value relationship to some other substitute product or products.

To demonstrate this point, we seldom see wheat offered at a price less than about 110 percent of the price of corn, and it usually is priced at about 115 percent of the price of the yellow grain. The reason is simple and sound: Wheat has a quite consistent nutritive advantage over corn. When the wheat price gets too close to the corn price, it makes better sense to buy the more expensive grain and feed it to animals. Although the per-bushel price for wheat will be greater, the feeding cost will be less, due to the superior nutriment in wheat. When this happens, of course, the oversupply that occasioned the low prices in the first place is consumed at an accelerated rate, and the wheat/corn ratio returns to a closer semblance of its historical relationship.

Similar examples can be cited throughout the commodity complex. So-called price/value ratios have been developed and are extensively used by traders around the world. A few of the better-known ones are: gold and silver, hogs and corn, wheat and oats, wheat and corn, soybeans and soybean oil and meal, beef and pork. The list is a long one.

We may be able to develop some kind of rationale concerning what constitutes a low price for a foodstuff, since we can assign costs for land, labor, and the equipment to produce a given product. Obviously, any price that returns less than the average costs of production and a fair profit is low by definition. But it is infinitely more difficult to settle on a definition of high price. Wheat may be selling at $5.00 per bushel—and this would be an historically high price. However, if corn was at $4.80 and oats at $4.20, wheat might appear to be significantly underpriced!

Any Price Can Be Right!

The purpose of this perhaps belabored discourse is to attempt to rid the reader's mind of any firm notions about what constitutes *high* prices or *low* prices. Most of the speculative tragedies are based on some kind of idea that a price has gone far enough. There may be some lower level where this kind of declaration can be made with relatively small risk, but *never* try to decide where high prices begin. The market is the only authority on this topic, and you will know it when sellers are willing to do business at lower levels—and buyers refuse to pay up for the supplies they want.

Infinite Supply and Demand

Unlike a cash market in produce, or a securities market, where the supply of a given article or stock is limited and perhaps well known, a futures market represents *unknown supplies.*

A certain corporation may have issued 5 million shares of stock. This is all of the shares available, and there can be no more unless the mechanics of an additional issue are completed according to law. Likewise, we may have a two-billion bushel soybean crop. Ignoring carryover, this is all of the soybeans we will have for a year's use—until the next harvest—unless foreign beans are brought in. Armed with this information, a trader in the common stock or in cash soybeans can attempt to equate fixed supplies with demonstrated historical demand. He may not succeed in developing an equation that will lead to a profit, but at least he can try.

In commodity futures speculation, there are no real or theoretical limits to the number of bushels or tons or carloads of the merchandise that may be "open" in the futures market at any time. So long as there are those who are willing to sell futures contracts, and others who are willing to buy at the market price, the total open-interest may represent twice the amount of the cash crop—or 10 times or 100 times its projected harvest volume. The only invariable is that for every buyer there must be a seller. And of course—at some price—there always is. Hence, the only limitation on the number of commodity contracts that may be open in the market at any point in time is the willingness and financial ability of buyers and sellers to undertake and maintain the specialized obligations involved at various price levels.

Futures Are Tied to Reality

The foregoing paragraph, taken at face value and with no further qualification, would seem to come close to declaring futures prices to be a sort of market-manufactured fiction. So now let's look at the economic ties that bind futures prices to the realities of *actual supply* and *actual demand*.

A commodity contract, unlike a share of stock or a piece of land, has a definite life span. A share of stock or a piece of real estate may approach immortality, since both can be passed from holder to holder through a succession of generations. In contrast, a commodity contract almost never has a trading life of more than two years, and most agricul-

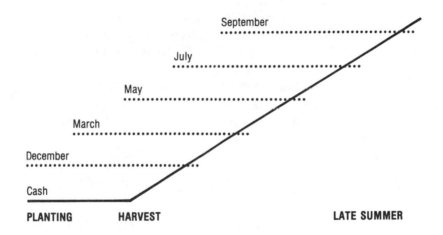

Chart 6-2

Trading in futures contracts goes on in every month of the year and, in most commodities, involves half a dozen or so contracts open for trade on any given day. However, each individual contract has a fixed life span, usually covering some 12 to 18 months.

In commodities categories that involve distinct patterns of seasonality in production and/or consumption, vastly different characteristics will be found in the several traded maturities.

For example, an old-crop contract (representing supplies available at the end of a crop year) may reflect extreme shortage, while the next contract out may evidence great surplus. The difference, of course, rests on expectations for a harvest that will come to market between the two contract maturities. The old-crop situation need not bear any resemblance to new-crop conditions, since each successive production year is a new problem in supply and demand.

So-called seasonal curves in certain commodities do not appear with anything like equal impact in all of the contracts traded. As a consequence, a trader should familiarize himself with the personality of the contracts he deals in—as well as getting to know the behaviorisms of the people against whom he must compete for profits.

tural commodities are traded in contracts that have a trading life of slightly less than one year.

When the last trading day in a contract has arrived and the bell has rung signaling expiration, every "short" who remains with an open position must make delivery of the physical commodity. He must deliver it within the location, time period, and quality standards set forth in the contract rules.

Every remaining "long" must accept the deliveries represented in his open contracts and pay for the cash merchandise in full on delivery.

As a consequence, a futures contract only represents a trade obligation until the contract expires, and it can be offset at any time the holder wishes to do so. However, if the contract is held to expiration, the bell that signals the end of trading in it also marks its transformation from an obligation to the physical commodity. Once trading has ended, delivery is mandatory. And since for every buyer there must be a seller, the number of contracts the remaining shorts must deliver are exactly matched by the number of contracts of the cash article that remaining longs must accept and pay for.

Viewed in this light, it must be apparent that futures prices can't possibly be presumed to live a life of their own. Futures contracts represent physical commodities throughout the trading life of the contract, and they *become* physical commodities on expiration of the contract. Necessarily, then, all of the fundamental considerations that apply to actuals also apply to futures. More than this, a day arrives when there is no tomorrow—when the trader must either offset or be prepared to deliver or take delivery. There is a moment of truth in the bull ring, and something like it also exists in the commodity pit when a maturity expires.

Cash and Futures Prices Converge

On the last day of trading, when the commodity represented in a contract must be offset or delivered in cash merchandise, the contract and the cash article are clearly one and the same—give or take a few days to handle the matter of physical delivery. Consequently, the price of the cash commodity and the expiring futures contract must also be practically the same.

The consideration that governs this phenomenon is:

> Rule: Cash price and the futures price will converge in the market on the last day of trading in an expiring contract.

Regardless of the premium that the cash item may command over the futures in periods of shortage during the life of the futures contract—and there is no real or theoretical limit to the extent of such an inversion—they will converge at expiration of the contract. Likewise, the price on the contract may reflect a condition of oversupply and show the full costs of carrying the commodity for the time period involved, which is the maximum premium over cash that is theoretically possible. But on the last day of trading, the convergence principle will have erased whatever "carrying charge" differential existed. Both *cash* and the *futures* prices will stand at precisely or virtually the same fraction of a cent as the contract goes off the board.

It is this price convergence principle, coupled with the tendency of cash and futures prices to follow each other, that makes hedging a protective as well as a profitable practice for dealers in physical inventories of the given commodity. A hedger knows that when the carrying-charge premium on a selected contract approaches the level of full carrying costs, she can profitably sell the contract against her inventory holdings. Price convergence guarantees her collecting the carrying-charge premium, provided she holds the dual market position to contract expiration. Should the normal carrying charge market turn into an inverted market, the hedger can theoretically stand to realize *any* amount of profit on her hedge. This, to repeat, is because there is no limit on the extent to which a price inversion or negative carrying charge may go, depending only on the seriousness of the shortage that precipitates it.

It must be remembered, however, that hedgers—like all of us who trade in the market—recognize it as a highly fluctuative affair. And the fluctuations involve not only flat prices, but price relationships, as well.

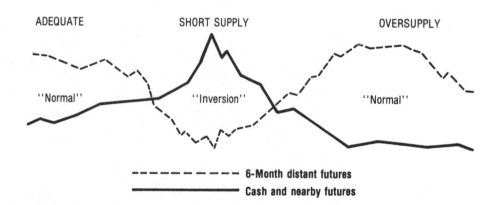

Chart 6–3

Shortages cause price inversions, and if the shortage is severe, the price inverse can be expected to reflect the full dimensions of the problem.

When a contract goes off the board, its maturity price will have found practically the same level as the price for the cash product in the selected market. Price convergence between maturing contracts and the corresponding contract grade of the cash article *must* take place, since maturity means delivery—and all remaining longs and shorts must now settle their obligations in actuals.

Rule: The premium that a more distant futures contract can reflect over a nearer contract, or the cash commodity, will never exceed the full costs of carrying the merchandise in storage for the time period involved. However, there is no limit to the premium that a nearby contract or the cash article may reflect over a more deferred contract.

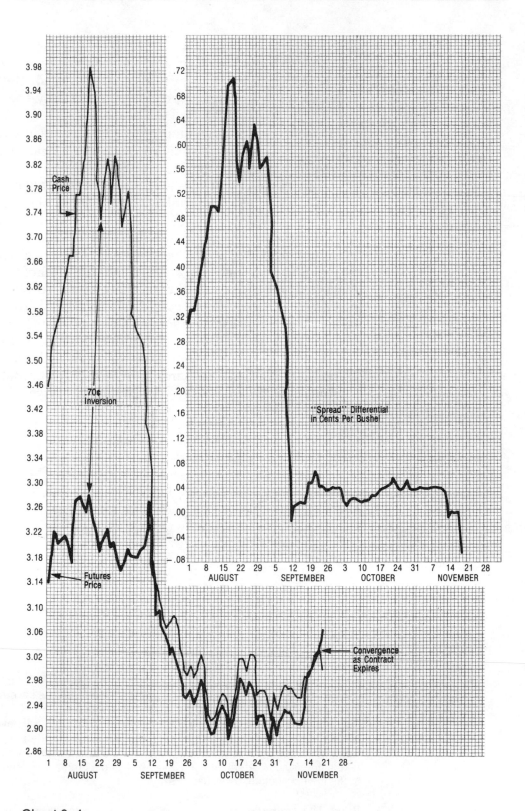

Chart 6-4

These charts show an admittedly extreme example of what can happen when demand
for a commodity outruns immediately available stocks of it. The chart to the left plots the

Chart 6–4 *(concluded)*

prices of cash soybeans and the futures contract separately. The chart inset to the right reflects the price differential in cents per bushel over the same time period.

It should be noted that, despite a tremendous 70 cent inversion in August, maturity found the November contract price and cash bids making a crossover. The contract finally went off the board at a slight premium to cash beans.

Also worthy of mention, the physical shortage of soybeans was by no means fully solved by mere expiration of the November contract. However, a more-than-ample harvest had laid all the fears of inadequate supplies to rest and changed market concern to one of what to do with an impressive surplus of the crop.

If a hedger, is *long* the cash and *short* the futures, he wants the differential, or basis, to narrow. If the hedger happens to be short the cash (by virtue of holding unfilled forward sales commitments) and long the futures, he wants the basis to widen. In either case, he stands to profit from his dual position to the extent that the *basis does change in his favor.* If, however, the basis on a hedge changes adversely, the hedger not only has failed to find the profit protection he sought, but he can also be a dollar loser on the hedge, in the bargain!

Recognizing these things, it should not be surprising to learn that hedgers often demonstrate a good bit of fancy footwork as they *place, lift,* and *shift* their hedges, which circumstances in their own businesses and profit opportunities in the market appear to warrant. Small wonder, then, that serious speculators expend important time and effort in attempting to analyze the hedgers' probable reaction to a given market situation.

Price Is a Many-Faceted Concept

It should now be clear that *price* can mean vastly different things to different segments of the market. To the average public trader, price usually relates to *flat price* for a trading unit of a selected commodity or futures. To the hedger, price almost always is a comparative value, quite consistently identified as a *basis on* or *off* (a premium over, or a discount off) a designated futures contract, or the cash article.

Among some large speculators whose trading inclines toward the holding of dual positions, long and short, between different contracts in the same commodity—or opposite positions in two or more commodities and/or products—price may be thought of and identified as a *spread* or *straddle.* The two terms, both of which mean the same thing, refer to a price difference between the two or more elements in the multiple position market posture being discussed.

If all of this has the effect of seeming to present price as a much more complicated concept than it appears to be on first encounter, then our objective has been met. Price *is* a complicated notion, presenting several facets to those who will take the time to study and learn to understand them.

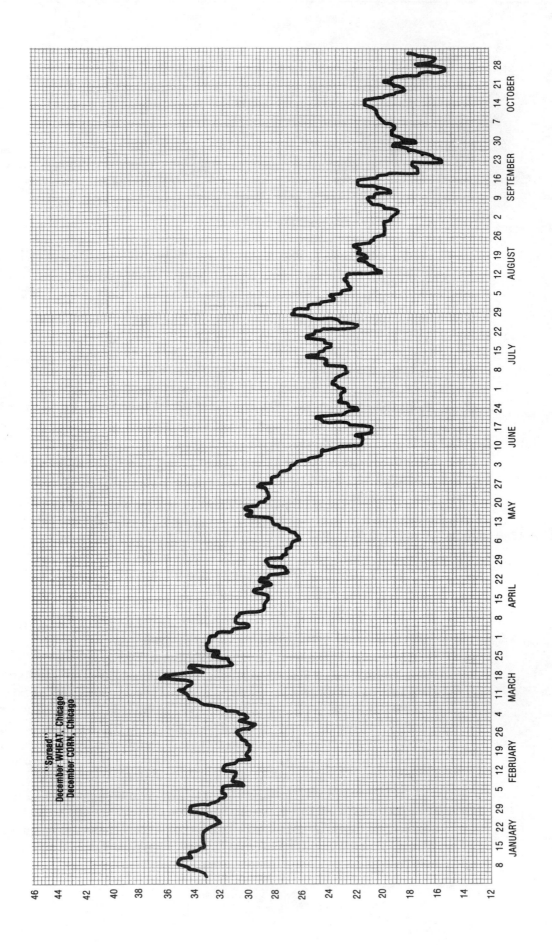

"Spread"
December WHEAT. Chicago
December CORN. Chicago

Chart 6-5

Commercial hedgers and traders who deal in spreads are vastly more concerned with price differentials than they are with flat prices.

This chart reflects the ever-changing pattern of price relationships between the December 1968 wheat and corn contracts. In March, the wheat futures held nearly a 37-cent premium over the corresponding corn maturity. By mid-September, the difference was down to about 15 cents. By being long December corn and short December wheat over that period, a spreader could have realized 22 cents on the basis change—regardless of how the individual contract prices rose or fell.

It is pertinent to note that, since the majority of new crop wheat is represented in the July contract and new crop corn is reflected in December, the corn/wheat basis is usually widest in late winter (when wheat stocks tend to be tight). The seasonal basis is historically narrowest in late summer (when the wheat glut is greatest, due to harvest pressures in the market).

The vast majority of all U.S. corn is fed to farm animals, rather than sold in the market. This usage pattern, which reflects a good deal of first-owner judgment can be sharply altered in the face of changing market prices—making corn a highly volatile commodity when supply/demand imbalances appear.

Wheat, being the preeminent grain in world trade, is much more affected by international considerations than is corn.

A lack of perspective about price has proven to be the root cause of untold speculative catastrophes. The price idea of the successful speculator goes far beyond the single figure level at which trade may take place. It includes, as well, the rationales under which all other important users of the market consider it. And to repeat again for emphasis, price must always be viewed as subject to sudden change, due to either altered fundamental factors which give rise to it or in reflection of revised trade psychology or technical stimulus, and with little or nothing to do with changes in supply/demand balance.

7

Understanding Trade
Volume as
a Measurement
of Urgency

If supply and demand find a point of equilibrium and remain in some close semblance of balance, we can expect only slight changes in price. It takes the stimulus of supply/demand *im*balance to move the price of any freely traded commodity into significantly higher or lower ground— and keep it there. Once the market has found its "right" price level, based on fundamental considerations, the new price/value appraisal can only be expected to persist (within a discernible trading range) until some further adjustment appears to revise price opinion anew.

Wait for Some Signs of Life

Depending on the breadth of the fluctuative range in a situation of supply/demand balance, the trading opportunities may be limited or nil, or they may be deemed actually negative. For example, Chart 7–2 reflects a situation in which the best a trader can hope for is about a 15-cent gross profit, so long as the price remains within its clearly defined channel. Hedgers, spreaders, and some large position speculators may find the long-term promise of a contract like this to be attractive, but for the average trader, who tends to think somewhat shorter-range, taking a position in such a contract would be ill-advised. Even if he succeeded in cashing in on the full fluctuative move, by the time he deducted broker commissions, his trading profit would be microscopic.

It is due to just such considerations that narrowly fluctuating contracts usually show unimpressive open-interest and trade volume. Most

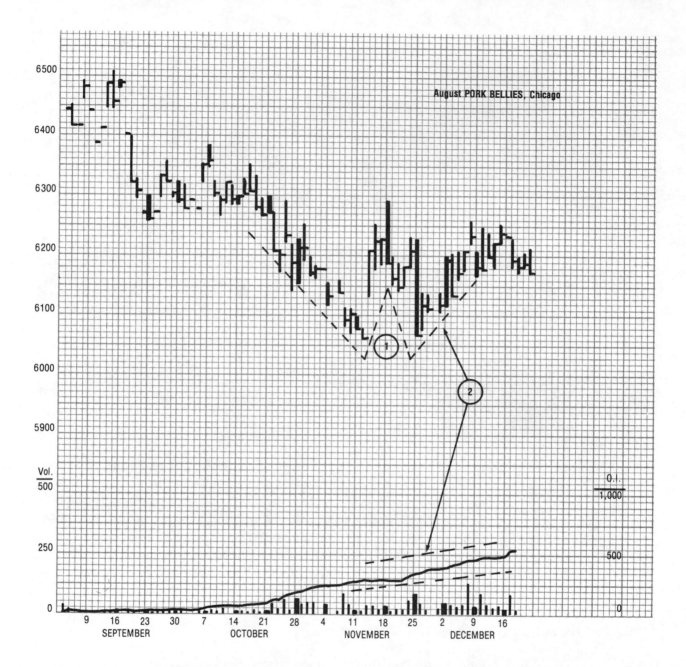

Chart 7-1

Technical market indicators are rarely to be trusted until sufficient open-interest and daily trade volume has built up in the contract to provide a reliable "tone" in the struggle between bulls and bears. However, this double bottom (1) and the triple signal that appeared in November and December (2) marked the beginning of an 800-point upward march.

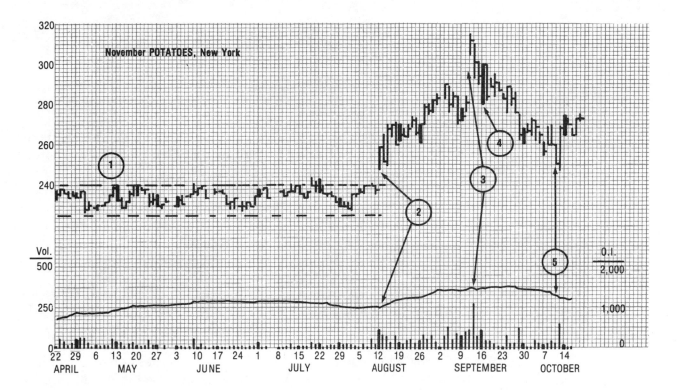

Chart 7-2

The holder of a position in this November potatoes contract needed both patience and money to wait the market out. For some eight months it remained a see-saw proposition, with little to excite either bulls or bears. Then suddenly it woke up.

On August 12th, price left the old trading range (1) with a leap of more than 10 cents per cwt., creating a gap (2) that was never to be filled. Longs and shorts joined the fray in impressive numbers, as the open-interest shows—and it was the bulls' initiative, all the way to 315.

The 25-cent jump on the opening of September 12 (3) was too much for the shorts' morale to withstand. They offset in waves throughout the next two sessions, and nervous longs also decided it was time to take profits rather than to try to press higher (4). Open-interest dipped on big volume, and the bull move was over.

Open-interest held up very well through the last half of September and the first week of October, and the bears were now in the driver's seat. When interest sagged and volume fell on October 7 to 10 (5), the technical conditions for a reversal were set—and it came the very next day.

It is germane to point out that the longs had to absorb some 60 cents impairment from the move before they succeeded in stemming the downtrend. This is far too long to wait for a reversal in hopes of eventually being saved by a turnaround.

speculators look for more price volatiltiy, and when they find it, both open-interest and trading volume climb in acknowledgment of the fact.

Price Change Attracts Interest

As has been said elsewhere, price must be viewed by the technical trader as a *cause*, even though the fundamentalist and the classical economist both consider it an *effect*. The technician knows that the market dynamics measured by open-interest and trade volume are triggered by price change. Moreover, the technician knows that unless a sleeping market is awakened by significantly higher or lower price, it can slumber right through to its last trading day. Profit-minded traders want no part of such a situation; that ties up speculative capital with no real chance for a good return on the position.

It is among the safest statements to aver that the biggest trade volumes are posted in connection with big price movements. As the price on a contract soars or plunges, half of the position holders are certain to be in trouble. Their scramble to move out of the path of increasing losses is equally certain to boost the level of trade in the session or sessions in which such an event occurs. And the exploding volume rate will not abate until the departing longs or shorts have found the safety of the sidelines.

It must, at this point, be emphasized that trading volume is a highly relative thing. For example, the volume in copper will usually be large multiples of the daily trade in silver, and the number of wheat contracts changing hands in a single session may exceed the total trading volume in oats or rye for a full month. Thus, the technical analyst must never fall into the trap of reading significance into a single piece of volume data. He must, instead, direct his attention to comparative changes in trading volume—either higher or lower—from what he sees to be the normal rate. Generally speaking, as long as daily volume remains fairly constant, it is a neutral factor. Only when it surges upward, or drops sharply, do we need to probe carefully behind the event to find the cause. *And the cause will usually be a change in price.*

All Holders Eventually Get Out

It has been stated previously that every long-holder is a potential seller, and every short-holder is a potential buyer. The open-interest figure will tell you how many contracts exist to be bought or sold for offset, now or at some time in the future, depending on what price does. You will make no error of consequence in viewing the entire open-interest as being eligible for offset, since at most only 1 to 2 percent of it stands any chance of being closed out through delivery. Of course, as a contract nears maturity, the amount of product that will be delivered in settlement be-

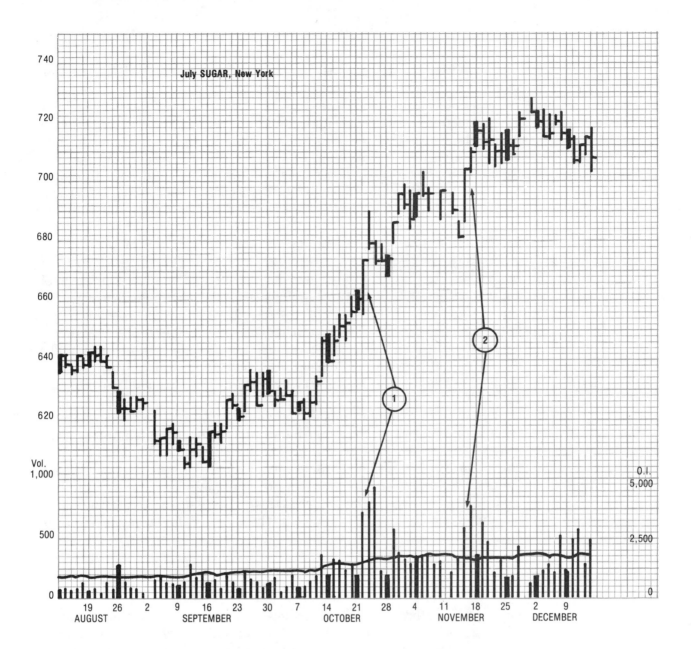

July SUGAR, New York

Chart 7-3

This chart demonstrates how long suffering the losers can be, as long as their losses come gradually. However, when a sudden jolt appears in price action (like that of October 22, 23, 24 (1) or that of November 14 and 15 (2), the departing holders of the wrong side of the contract can make new volume records.

Open-interest data tells us that in both of the above-cited instances, new bears stepped up to take the place of those who went to the sidelines. Had the departing short-losers not been replaced, the necessary financing for higher prices would not have existed, and any of the three distinct short-squeezes that occurred in October and November could have been reversal points.

Open-interest data is indispensable in analyzing the near-term implications of this kind of price behavior. Without it, the trader can blunder into a price trap, purely on the basis of a new high that means nothing in itself.

comes a larger part of the diminishing open-interest that remains in the last few days of trading.

However, for our purposes of discussion, we can safely say that most, if not all, of the current open positions in any given contract will be closed out by offset if the proper kind of price stimulus develops. There is a progressive scale upon which every long holder *must* take his loss and offset in the face of lower prices. In the opposite frame of reference, there is also a scale upon which even the stoutest short *must* run for cover in the face of higher prices. Even if courage outlasts prudence, financial resources will eventually be depleted—and that's the end to it.

In any kind of a squeeze, trade volume tends to be swollen by the scalper function in the pits. As frantic shorts are forced to buy back their impaired positions (at higher prices), it is usually the pit scalpers who will provide the needed contracts initially. The scalpers, in turn, hope to be able to offset (buy them back) later, and at a lower price level. Or, when it is the long contingent who need relief, the scalpers are usually ready to accommodate them (at lower prices), hoping to resell the contracts later at a higher price. In either case, if a scalper is the man on the other side of an offset trade, he is almost certain to be a short-term holder of the position. Scalpers, it should be remembered, rarely carry positions overnight. They trade extremely short-term for small profits on a big volume.

So, if a public trader offsets a position with a pit scalper, the contract is almost certain to change hands at least once more before the end of the session, since the scalper will try to be out of the position before the closing bell rings. As a consequence, in a lively market, each open contract being offset can pass from the public holder through one—or several—successive scalping trades, before it finally comes to the hands of someone who wants to maintain the position for a day, a week, or longer.

Price Changes Trigger Volume

Volume, therefore, must be considered to be more a measurement of trading velocity than it is of the sheer number of contracts changing hands. You may even encounter situations in which the daily volume on a contract is greater than the total open-interest in the same contract. It sounds like a contradiction in terms until we remember that each traded contract can theoretically pass through dozens of hands in the course of a day's trading, without adding a single digit to the open-position figure.

Anytime volume surges, look first to price for the cause. The primary question to be answered is, "Who is in trouble?" If it appears that open-interest has been steadily building over a period of time marked by a rather gradual price movement, you can expect that the stop-losses may be equally well dispersed. In such a case, the smallest technical correction may set off a chain-reaction effect, carrying a good way before all of the disenchanted longs or shorts are stopped out. However, should

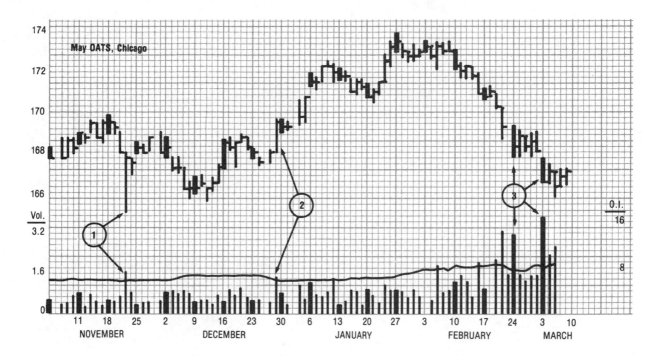

Chart 7-4

Examination of this chart will show how very closely the technicians watch price behavior in some of the so-called small markets.

Oats is rarely a widely-swinging commodity. Its open-interest is characteristically modest, and its volume equally restrained. However, a price move that would get no attention in wheat, corn, or soybeans, can trigger a wide assortment of fireworks in the oats pit. The price drop (1) on November 21 is a fine demonstration of what happens when a lot of holders try to get out, all at the same time. The liquidity factor is crucial when it comes times to offset!

Also, note the volume reaction (2) to the fractional-cent new interim high on December 27. Clearly, a large bunch of stop-orders overhung the market at almost precisely the old $1.69 level. On February 24 and March 3, we again see (3) volume blossoming, but price holds to a modest range. We must conclude that the stop-loss orders to sell were well matched by buy-orders from shorts taking profits.

---

a distinct price "step" exist in the chart, be extremely wary of pressing either long or short activities as price approaches the obvious level at which large numbers of bunched stop-orders can be expected to rest.

Anticipating the Squeeze Pattern

The usual chain of events in a technical move is for volume to pick up dramatically as the first stop-orders are hit, stay at a high level until the weak hands are chased out, and then go suddenly quiet. When the volume of trade dries up following either a sharp run-up or a price slide, a turnaround is usually ready to begin.

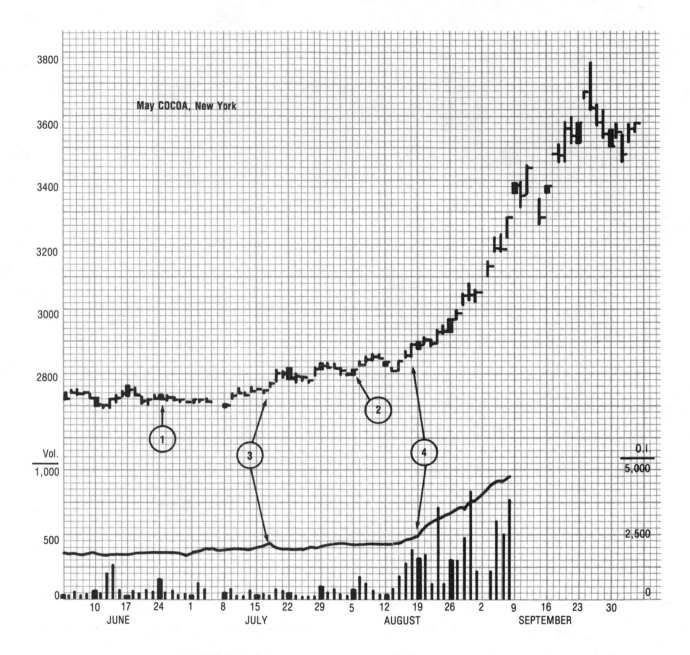

Chart 7-5

Trading a price pattern like this can present some difficulties in the placement of protective stop-orders. 2700 looks crucial for the downside until about mid-July (1). But it isn't until August that a discernible "step" appears as a probable stop-point for both longs and shorts (2).

It is in situations of this kind that randomly placed resting-orders can be touched off by a price surprise and carry for great distances—like a *trail* of gunpowder—as compared to *clusters* placed at intervals.

The indicators signaled the direction of this market (3) on the 16th and 17th of July and confirmed the coming bull move again during the week of August 12 (4). A market of this kind is maintaining extremely fine technical tone, indicative of a commercial trade. Strong hands are on both sides of the situation, and it is they who are creating the "personality" of this kind of finely tuned contract.

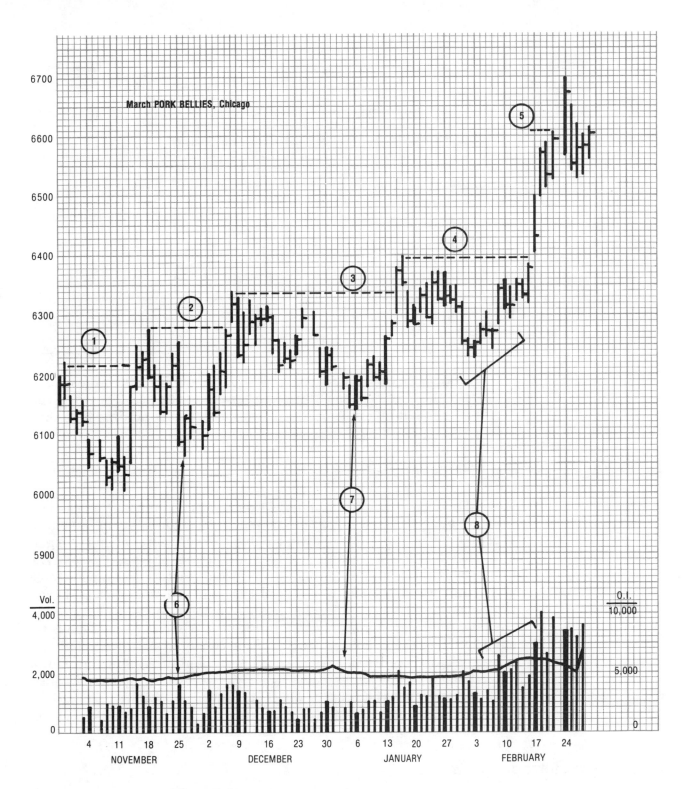

March PORK BELLIES, Chicago

Chart 7-6

There should be little reason for questions about the sensitive price levels in a chart like this one. Well-defined stair steps offer attractive points for the losers to "give up"—and for the winners to "double up." (*continued on next page*)

Chart 7–6 *(concluded)*

Note the amazing consistency with which each upside resistance level (1-2-3-4-5) is passed on big volume (indicating some degree of short-squeezing), but nearly every time, a sharp downside correction takes place as soon as the weak shorts have run.

Pork bellies is a commodity in which speculation far exceeds the commercial hedging being done. As a consequence, we would expect to see a somewhat higher degree of short-term price volatility. However, another fact is equally well revealed: A high proportion of belly traders are chartists. As a result, these *form traders* tend to make similar decisions, thus producing a chart that performs in a highly stylized fashion. The random decisions of speculators who put little store in chart tracings rarely reflect the disciplined geometrics found in contracts that attract large numbers of technicians.

Finally, to return to the chart, price course was signaled (6) at the end of November, (7) in early January, and (8) the second week in February. Throughout most of this charted period, the trade followed higher price but shunned price slides.

> Rule: never sell a quiet market after a price drop and never buy a quiet market after a price rise.

The opposite can't be stated with equal impunity, but professional traders make a lot of money by doing just the opposite: They *buy* the trading lulls that follow sharp price drops and *sell* the trading lulls that follow sharp price bulges.

Don't Expect Repeat Performances

A sudden drop in trading volume is every bit as significant as the impressive spurt that often precedes it. When the trade dries up, we know that those who were previously in trouble had every opportunity to get out. They either ran or chose not to run. *The urgency has passed.* We know that the weak hands probably conducted whatever stampede took place, and we also know that it will take somewhat higher or lower prices to frighten the same camp in days to come. Accept it as gospel that *the trade never worries about a price it has seen before.* This is to say that if someone holds a long position in sugar at 5 cents and the price goes to 4¾ cents, he may give serious thought to selling out. However, if he stays with it, 4¾ cents will never worry him again; 4½ cents may prompt him to sell out, or 4¼ cents, but he has been "vaccinated" against 4¾ cents by having lived through it once. It will never bother him again, as long as he holds this position.

50 Percent Retracements

When trade volume dries up following a significant price move, it is our signal that the *reaction* is probably the next stage. Whether we want to try to capitalize on it or not, we should expect a price reversal and have some notion about its probable amplitude. In this connection, many price chartists look for a 50 percent retracement in any major price

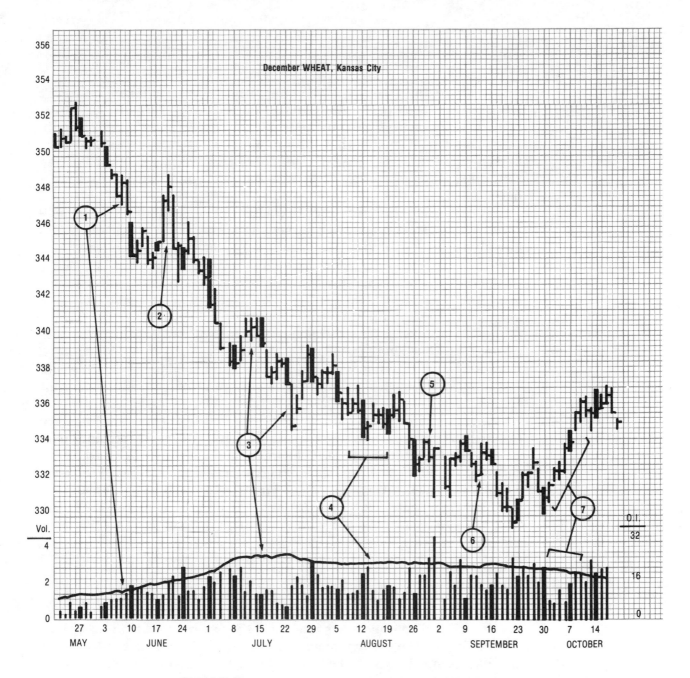

Chart 7-7

There was never a reason for a technician to wonder about the direction of this market. Open-interest and volume kept climbing through the last week of May and the first week of June, as prices moved steadily lower. A modest reversal (1) on June 6 put a dip in open holdings but produced no frenzy among the shorts. Even the four-cent bulge the week of June 17 was well absorbed by the shorts—and prices promptly broke back (2).

The four-day attempt to break over 3.41 failed, but the bull's effort reduced some contract interest and made the technical picture look like a turnaround could be in the making. However, when the bulls failed to run in the face of the 2-cent break (3) on July 22 and 23, it was clear that the losers were willing to finance still lower prices.

The longs waited out the resistance area between 3.36 and 3.32 (4), but when the price stopped at 3.34 two days in a row (5), the flight began, as evidenced in volume.

Another small rally that failed at 3.34 discouraged some of the longs (6), and interest loss shows it. The rest of the weak longs left on the new low price of September 20, providing the technical strength required for a turnaround. The market after September 30 (7) was loath to follow the higher prices; hence, after the weak shorts were taken out on the bulge, the trend turned down once more.

move. There seems to be as many instances where the formula doesn't work as there are where it does, but the 50 percent retracement phenomenon has an excellent basis in the technical trading behavior of the public speculator. We know that losing bulls always finance lower prices, and losing bears always bankroll higher prices. We also know that when the supply of these victims dries up, so does the price move they are underwriting.

At the top or bottom of any price pattern, the last buyers or last sellers of the contract begin with immediate losses. The professionals will abandon their impaired positions in short order, but an established attitude dies hard, so even some of these experienced traders will be looking for an opportunity to get back in at some better (higher or lower) price level. Less experienced hands will be merely holding on, hoping that the price will return to a point where they can get out without loss. Others of faulty judgment or a self-destructive bent will see an opportunity to average up on a short position by selling more; or average down on a long position by buying more. There is no faster road to speculative ruin than averaging, even though a few visionaries do insist that it works for them.

As events unfold and the trouble persists, even the most bright-eyed optimist must eventually recognize reality. The more precipitously price moves against the losers, the more anxious they will be to offset. But if price moves slowly to their disadvantage, it is remarkable how heroically they will withstand the economic agony of being eaten an inch at a time. It usually takes a good deal of adversity to convince the losers they are wrong, and a 50 percent retracement is perhaps as good an estimate as any other.

Key Reversal

As this kind of charade plays itself out, the experienced traders will begin looking for the justly famous *key reversal day*. In a nutshell, this is a trading session in which the last contingent of die-hard losers come to see the hopelessness of their situation. Something happens to sink their last vestige of hope, and they begin offsetting. Price soars or plunges to a new contract high or low, and trading volume goes even higher. Suddenly, as quickly as the conflagration began, trade may come almost to a standstill. The pit traders are usually the first to recognize this symptom, and the scalpers who hold positions at the end of the price move now are doing the unloading.

Eventually volume begins to pick up once more, but price is now headed in the opposite direction from that of a few minutes ago. And if it is to come onto the chart as a fully trustworthy reversal, the closing price for the session will be *significantly* higher or lower than the preceding day's close.

A price reversal, of course, was precisely what the disadvantaged longs or shorts were looking for all the time. But as long as there were enough losers left to finance another step up or down on the price scale,

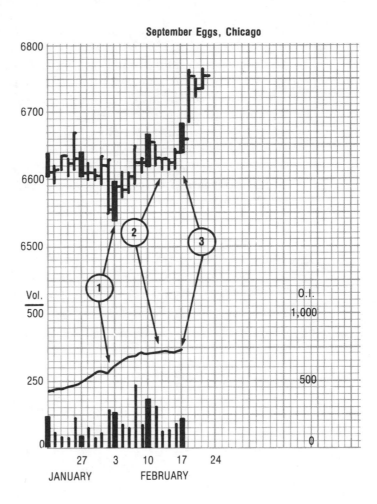

Chart 7-8

There should not have been an egg chartist anywhere who failed to spot the *key reversal* (1) that took place on February 3: a new low price on big volume, followed by a sharply higher price and a close well above the close of the previous session.

Then, after signaling the upturn, the chart went on to reflect price, volume, and open-interest all rising together. Volume dried up (2) on the minor price set-back of February 12 and 13, and it climbed (3) with the bulge on the 14th and 17th, along with an increase in open holdings. This kind of clear-cut direction won't appear often, but it does occur often enough to give the technician a thumping advantage over those who ignore indicators.

In about three weeks, the bulls took some 3 cents out of their long positions.

---

the reversal was technically out of the question. Only after the *blowoff* are the technical factors set to carry price in the opposite direction.

In summation of this section, it must now be said that volume is a sphinx most of the time. Weeks or months may pass during which this indicator will hardly evidence a noticeable change. Then, for reasons that not even the most devoted market watcher can discern, the contract will begin to come alive—as measured in trade volume. It is not important that you understand all of the facts behind a change in the vital signs of a commodity contract. In point of fact, it may be better if you are somewhat in the dark. The market rarely pays a trader for reading the newspaper, and if you know what underlies a notable change in market health, so do several thousand others. And if this is the case, don't try to trade on the information. Chances are that the market has already discounted it!

The expert market technician tries to keep his approach as simple as possible. He attempts to deal only with those things that are measurable and predictable. Price, volume, and open-interest are all measurable, and traders are predictable.

You need nothing else to succeed in speculation.

8

Understanding Open-Interest as a Measurement of Conflicting Opinions

It has already been pointed out that for every buyer there must be a seller, and this is, of course, true in every facet of trade. However, *short-seller* conjures up a distinct kind of image in the minds of most of us. Semantically, the term suggests that the seller does not have whatever it is that she has sold. Hence, the implication seems to be that if events require her to make delivery to her buyer, doing so might prove difficult—or perhaps even impossible. Since delivery is only one means of contract settlement, the hazards are more imagined than real.

In the securities market, there are those who do a substantial amount of short-selling, involving stock that has been borrowed from brokers. Since stock exists in a limited supply, before one sells it short, he must be sure that he has located or arranged for enough shares to meet his commitment if need be. However, short-interest in the securities market seldom exceeds 2 percent of the total of all shares outstanding.

In the commodity futures markets, *short-interest* is always exactly equal to *long-interest*. It cannot be otherwise. Futures markets involve dealing in obligations calling for deferred performance. The long holder of a contract of May cocoa can't get delivery of the commodity until the designated delivery period, regardless of how badly he may want it at an earlier date. By the same token, the holder of a short position in the same futures contract cannot make delivery until the contract calls for it. As a consequence, it is seen that both the long and the short have no choice except to wait for *first notice day*, or either or both may offset at any time they wish to do so before expiration of the contract.

Disagreement Makes Markets

In view of the foregoing, it should be seen that *open-interest is a measurement of the willingness of longs and shorts to maintain opposing positions in the market.* In another sense, open-interest in a contract or a commodity is a quantitative indicator of the difference of opinion that exists between market participants as to the direction price will move. It must be conceded that the speculative long would not buy and hold a position unless he expected the price to improve. The speculative short that holds the other side of the position must be equally sure that lower prices will eventuate to his advantage. Unless *both* are convinced that their appraisal of things to come is the correct one, the long and the short that are required to add one open contract to total open interest would simply not exist as an added pair.

In such a case, if the new bull wants to buy he will have to obtain his contract or contracts from an old long who stands ready to sell and offset—and allow someone else to take his place as the long-side holder of an already existing open contract. If the new bull is anxious to obtain a position and he can only find reluctant sellers, he will likely have to acquire the contract or contracts he wants at some higher price level. At *some* price there is bound to be a seller.

When a new bear arrives, he can only expect to place his offering with a new bull or an offsetting short position holder who is now ready to let someone else replace him as the open holder of part or all of his commitments in the contract concerned.

Multiply these individual decisions by hundreds or thousands of traders, and you have the mechanics by which open-interest increases, remains constant, or declines. As somewhat of a tripartite axiom, conceded to be more mechanical than economic, the following conclusions can be generally drawn from open-interest data.

1. When open-interest increases, present holders are increasing their positions, or new holders are joining them on both sides of the contract. The quantitative difference of opinion as to the course of price is growing.
2. When open-interest holds steady, new holders are replacing those who offset, or existing strong hands may be taking up the contract holdings of the weak hands that are abandoning their positions in the face of losses.
3. When open-interest declines, weak handed holders are offsetting in the face of adverse price movement or spurred by impatience. Their offerings to buy or sell are, to some extent, being taken up by the holders who earlier constituted the other side of the contracts now being liquidated. Quantitative difference of opinion is, in this situation, decreasing.

Small Conflicts May Suffice

Since speculation is pursued by different people for different reasons, and with different profit or loss-avoidance objectives in mind, the differ-

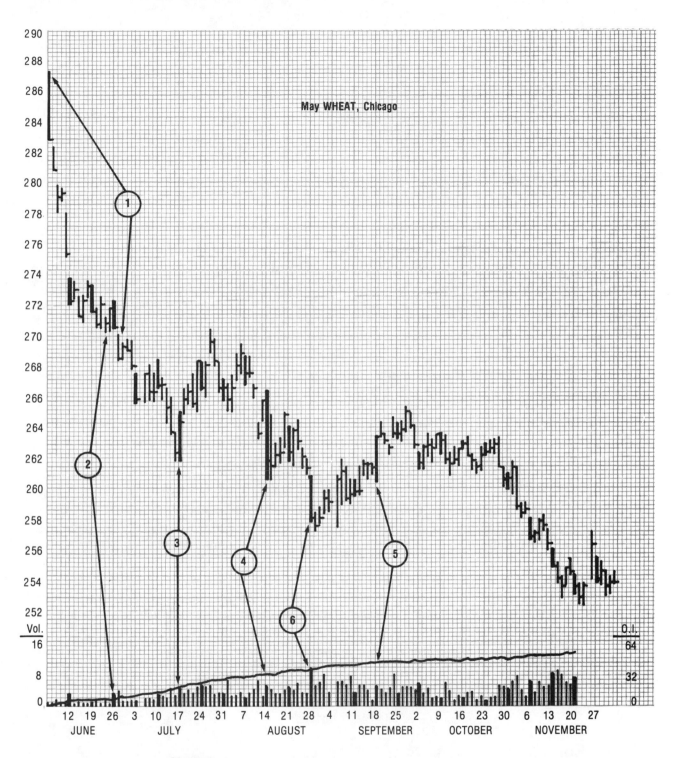

Chart 8-1

There are situations, like this May wheat, where the technical indicators offer little guidance. Open-interest in this contract merely continued to grow, regardless of whether price was trending up or down. It is clear that traders were reluctant to do business in the range down from 2.87¼ to 2.70 (1). However, once the price stuck on a 2.70½ low two days in a row (2), open-interest began to climb—and it never met an appreciable setback for five months.

Note how the major price moves of July 17 (3), August 14–15 (4), and September 18 (5) all fail to elicit anything that could be considered "squeeze volume." August 28 (6) comes

Chart 8-1 (*concluded*)

closest to the appearance of weak hands running for the sidelines. The question to be answered is, "Why didn't the losers run?" The answer is very clear.

Wheat was in a major bear trend during the period covered by this chart. Public traders want to be long, hence they could not get a comfortable trade in wheat. The holders in this contract, both long and short, were, for the most part, hedgers or spreaders—trading on price differentials rather than flat prices. These holders were able to virtually ignore individual price moves on this contract, as long as the basis price on their dual positions behaved in a satisfactory fashion.

Of course there were some net-shorts and some net-longs in the contract also, but the spread considerations took overwhelming precedence over everything else.

---

ences of opinion that will prompt taking a position in a futures contract need not be very great. For example, a hedger who buys or sells a commodity futures position may have no real interest in what the flat price on the futures does. He is primarily seeking an opposite stance in the contract to the one he holds in a cash commodity inventory. His profit hopes are tied exclusively to a change in the price differential between the two sides of the hedging position. Moreover, a lot of companies hedge almost automatically for protection against loss in inventory value that could result from a change in market price. Profit on the hedge is, in the minds of these market users, a secondary consideration, their first concern being the avoidance of possible loss.

Those rapid-fire pit traders that the market identifies as scalpers are quite content to buy and sell for a small fraction of a cent per bushel or a few pennies per ton. Their profit expectations are modest as concerns any particular trade, but they multiply small profits by a huge trading volume—and the final result can be most pleasing.

Day traders who operate on the floors of the exchanges are also satisfied with small profits and settle for modest price moves rather than carry positions overnight.

The large speculators that are often called *position traders,* are regularly looking for big returns. In order to get the maximum profit from a position, they are willing to carry it for weeks or months—as long as the price behaves within their limits of risk toleration.

Public traders are perhaps the greediest of all. It's hard to find a newcomer to the market who is without his dream of a quick fortune. Some have found the almost instant wealth they were looking for, and such tales will always prompt others to try to find the path and follow in the footsteps of the big winners.

It Takes Both Bulls and Bears

With such a wide variation of profit expectations reflected by those who trade, it is not surprising to discover that most markets always offer opportunities to buy and sell at least a contract or two in quite close proximity to the "last tick." The initial difference of opinion that will produce the buyer and seller required to open another contract may be almost microscopic. Should the pair be a scalper and a hedger, an eighth

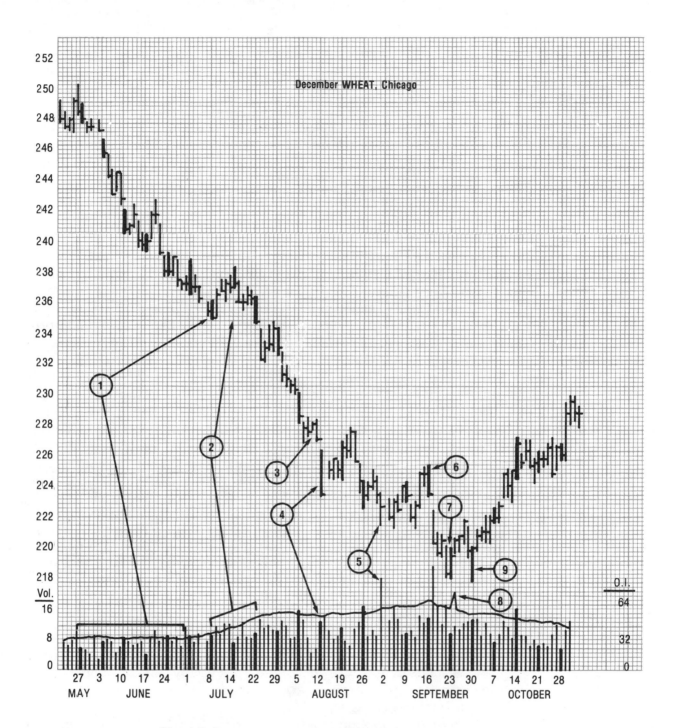

Chart 8-2

To emphasize the difference of "personalities" in different contracts of the same commodity, let's now examine this December wheat chart. Keep in mind that this is a different crop year than the May contract portrayed in Chart 8–1.

Open-interest and volume remained quite level, as bulls and bears followed price down to 2.35 (1). The 2-week bulge (2) in July increased the interest in the contract substantially, and it continued to grow until the slight bulge (3) and a 3-3/8 cent break on August 12 (4) convinced both bulls and bears that a turnaround was likely.

The shorts cashed profits on the squeeze of August 30 (5) or sweated out a 4 cents loss to September 16 (6). *(cont.)*

Chart 8-2 (*concluded*)

September 23 (7) was a huge *bull trap.* The new low and a higher close developed, but volume was much too small to be a blowoff. Eager bulls brought in, and the bears let them have it. Open-interest soared (8) on September 24, but it fell just as fast when the move was not sustained on the 25th.

Weak-handed longs were chased out on the new contract low (9) of September 30, and now the technical elements were set to support an upside move.

Note: Anyone who gave decent regard to trade volume would have seen the bull trap of September 23 as a phoney climax. Key reversals that can be trusted *never* take place on low volume. Always be suspicious of a quiet trade turnaround. It will be a false move more often than not.

---

or a quarter of a cent will doubtless be enough to make the trade. But *both* must see some kind of profit (or protection) opportunity; or the trade will not be made.

For an impressive open-interest to build up in a contract, however, there must be a large and confident herd of bulls that expect an impressive price rise. Opposite them, we must have an equally aggressive contingent of bears who are unflinching in their opinion that the price will fall. As these opponents join the fray in ever-increasing numbers, the central issue always remains the same, but the market pressures—and sensitivities—grow tremendously.

A foremost consideration is the fact that every position holder is a creature of emotions. He has several courses of action open to him minute by minute, as the sequence of events in the life of the contract unfold: He can maintain his position, add to it, reduce it, or close it out completely. And the course he follows will be dictated exclusively by what he considers to be his *own* best interests. Speculation has been called the loneliest business in the world; everybody faces his own risks and chooses from the available alternatives—alone. A friendly broker or a well-intentioned contemporary may offer sympathy or suggestions, but the trader must still sink or swim on the basis of his own decisions.

Price Agreement Reduces Interest

As long as the issue of which way price is headed is unresolved, open-interest tends to hold its own or increase. But any time the traders think they have found an interim answer to the question, open-interest always shrinks in acknowledgment of it.

Difference of opinion builds open-interest, and consensus reduces it. Regardless of which direction price is moving, someone is being hurt. When losses occur, depend on it: Some of the losers are closing out their positions. Others may be joining the disadvantaged camp at a fast enough pace to keep the open-interest graph steady, or even rising. But, that losses produce offsets is as safe as any market maxim can be. Moreover, if enough of the weak-handed initial holders are replaced by newcomers with the right combination of conviction and financial muscle, the price trend may be halted and turned around. Such a feat won't last long, unless the fundamentals justify it. But it can be done.

Winners May Also Run from Price

Losers aren't the only ones that may run in the face of a price move; winners also have some interests at stake. If an important segment of those on the profitable side of the contract should decide that the move to a higher or lower level can't be trusted, they may decide to take their profits and move to the sidelines. When this happens, open-interest shrinks for the obvious reason that when the longs or shorts run in the face of losses and the opposite-side holders close their positions out of choice, *both* are merely executing equal-and-opposite transactions to the ones that established their positions initially. They are offsetting each other, and the contracts they held are now being taken off the open-interest roster.

When both longs and shorts seem agreed that a price move is going too far or in the wrong direction, a turnaround is at least an extremely ripe probability. A shrinking of open-interest is your best clue to a reduction in the difference of opinion that must *always* underpin a price move, if it is to remain intact. When total contract holdings begin falling off, both the winners and the losers are suffering from cold feet. Extreme caution is called for, because markets that show this kind of symptom are, at best, highly questionable affairs.

Most of the traders who have had the unfortunate experience of being caught in the wildly swinging reversals of the market whip-saw could have saved themselves the punishment. Heed the warning contained in falling open-interest, when it follows on the heels of a substantial price move in either direction. It tells you that vacillation prevails in the winners' camp, and a price reversal is the best probability in sight.

Be Suspicious of Thin Markets

If for no other consideration except liquidity, the prudent trader should try to seek out the well-traded contracts. Anyone who has had the frustrating and costly experience of trying to get an order filled in a *thin* market should need no lecture on the benefits of trading the big ones. Open-interest is your best guarantee of a continuing high degree of liquidity, and only liquidity can save you from having to pay up on your purchases and sell down on your sales.

Thin trading situations can sometimes offer an eye-popping brand of price fireworks, but the prudent speculator is not seeking mere excitement. He's looking for profits above all else, and to find them he needs a trade situation with the highest possible degree of predictability. The larger the crowd in a selected contract and the more clearly defined they are in terms of being weak hands or strong hands, the better the prospects for the technician.

Leave the small, explosive situations for those who really believe in luck. They will need it!

9

Understanding Trade Mix as a Division of Market Forces

It is most difficult, and it may be impossible, to talk about the relative quality of market judgments without bruising the sensibilities of many of those very people that this volume is intended to help. Certainly, no writer opens up new ground by merely pointing out that the public is usually wrong in its market judgments. Entire trading programs are based essentially on the reliability of always assuming that the public will point itself in the wrong direction in most, if not all, of the markets in which it trades.

But even the most defensible generality has points of great weakness. And the unqualified portrait of the public trader as a kind of perennial "Wrong Way Corrigan" of the market place is beginning to lose credence among those who have nothing to hazard by admitting the fact. Increased information is the one thing that will improve the trading effectiveness of an individual—regardless of his category. In commodity markets, especially, the amount and quality of information broadly disseminated to the public—although still much too sparse to be considered fully ample—is improving at an impressive rate. To state it another way, the informational advantage that the large speculators and commercial interests have historically enjoyed over their smaller competitors is being surely and not-so-slowly taken away. Better statistics on the part of various agencies of government, as well as from highly skilled private sources, is only part of the improvement.

The great brokerage houses that, in time not long past, often shunned the small commodity speculator have now found that this category of business does have its economic attractions. And while the usefulness of the so-called market advice that emanates from the commission houses must at least be viewed with deep reservations, the general market data they provide their subscribers is at least good—and some of it deserves the grade of "excellent."

What Makes Weak Hands Weak

If this is the case, it might be asked, why does the small public trader merit the uncompromising label of *weak hands* in the commodity market? The answer is to be found not in the caliber of information *available* to him, but in his lack of a trading program and his consistent tendency to panic in the presence of limited dangers. For example, one steer can get full of loco weed and cause himself a good deal of difficulty as he runs amok. But when a thousand steers manifest the same behavior, it's a stampede—and the resulting damage may have to be calculated in geometric, rather than arithmetic terms.

The same thing is true in the market. The weak-handed public trader is weak because of what he does en masse, rather than because of who he is individually.

As soon as a public trader outgrows the herd instinct and learns to think for himself and control his emotions, he ceases to be a small trader, because he has mastered the rudiments required to make him large. He now must be taken out of the small-trader category, regardless of the size of his free balances with brokerage houses, because he no longer conducts himself as a small trader. And in doing so, he has qualified himself for the appellation of *strong hands*!

Some of the most consistently profitable traders are people who never hold more than a modest open position in a single commodity, unless profits from that position urge pyramiding. They stick to a settled trading program and refuse to be stampeded by either success or failure. They are willing to forego the possibility of making a quick million for the privilege of not having to contemplate an equally quick bankruptcy. Their prudence and self-discipline takes them out of the company of those who are endlessly tossed and buffeted by the whims of market circumstance. They know their objective and pursue it with the same purposefulness observed on the part of the large speculators and commercial interests.

Strong Hands

Size by itself is certainly a chancy index to either native intelligence or acquired knowledge, but in order to become a large factor in the market, an individual or a firm must be able to operate profitably. Profits are the only useful yardstick in measuring the relative effectiveness of the trading programs of the several classes of market participants. And the profit performance of the huge corporations that deal in food and fiber commodities is impressive, indeed. Since companies like Beatrice, General Mills, Quaker Oats, Kellogg, and Lever Bros. are continually hedging in futures markets, it must be assumed that hedging adds to their economic effectiveness. If this were not so, they would not do it. The central business engagement of these big commercial interests is the acquisition, merchandising, processing, and distribution of commodities and the products made from commodities. Hedging is not *another* business; it is—or ought to be—an integral part of *any* business that requires owning an inventory that is subject to value changes over time.

The hedger is usually credited with only a modest objective: to escape the risks inherent in price fluctuation. Most explanations of hedging suggest that a grain merchant can place a *perfect hedge,* and thereby freeze his normal profit opportunity by protecting himself against fluctuations in market price—either positive or negative. Even if so-called perfect hedges did exist, and they almost never do, finding one would fall far short of gladdening the heart of the hedger. Hedgers, like other businessmen, seek profit. The hedging operations, like other business profit centers, is expected to produce a profit. Since the practice of hedging persists on the part of commercial interests, we must conclude that the results of hedging are positive: that the protection being sought is more often than not found, and that the economic benefits (profits) are, on the average, greater than the economic penalties (losses).

If the above hypothesis is accepted—and it seems to be rebuttal-proof—then we must grant further that the results are a testimonial to the intelligence and sagacity with which hedgers conduct their market activities. Obviously, a bad trade will lose money for anyone who makes it. Only a good trade can show a profit, and only good traders can sustain the kind of profitability averages required to bring the affluence and increasing self-confidence that are the hallmarks of success in any economic endeavor.

Good Hedgers Are Great Traders

The commercial hedgers are, to run the risk of scrambling market labels, among the best *traders* in the market. This is to say that there is no category of market users that demonstrates a cooler judgment or a more critical appraisal of events to come than does the hedging group. True, the hedger operates from a significantly different frame of reference than the *spreader* or flat-price speculator, but all three must cope with the same price behavior and machinery of trade.

The commercial hedger operates without some of the limitations that obtain in the area of speculation, but it can also be argued that the hedger has his own unique market handicaps to balance things. For example, a hedger *must* trade in the market that exists if he is to continue to do business. A speculator has the valuable privilege of merely moving to the sidelines when the market looks less than attractive. A com-

Chart 9-1
Wheat—Chicago Board of Trade Commitments of Traders in All Futures Combined and Indicated Futures, August 31, 1984

		Reportable positions									
		Noncommercial								Nonreportable Positions	
	Total open interest	Long or short only		Long and short (spreading)		Commercial		Total			
		Long	Short	Long	Short	Long	Short	Long	Short	Long	Short
					(Thousand bushels)						
All	232,952	17,035	32,210	8,505	8,505	125,775	85,260	151,315	125,975	81,637	106,977
Old	227,277	19,460	32,210	6,080	6,080	125,775	84,215	151,315	122,505	75,962	104,772
Other	5,675	0	2,425	0	0	0	1,045	0	3,470	5,675	2,205
				Changes in commitments from July 31, 1984							
All	−13,613	−1,380	19,210	−5,835	−5,835	−4,025	−17,445	−11,240	−4,070	−2,373	−9,543
				Percent of open interest represented by each category of traders							
All	100.0%	7.3	13.8	3.7	3.7	54.0	36.6	65.0	54.1	35.0	45.9
Old	100.0%	8.6	14.2	2.7	2.7	55.3	37.1	66.6	53.9	33.4	46.1
Other	100.0%	0.0	42.7	0.0	0.0	0.0	18.4	0.0	61.1	100.0	38.9

	Total number of traders	Number of traders in each category									
All	104	15	28	10	10	34	40	54	75		
Old	104	15	28	8	8	34	40	54	73		
Other	4	0	2	0	0	0	2	0	4		

Concentration ratios
Percent of open interest held by the indicated number of largest traders

	By gross position				By net position			
	Four or less traders		Eight or less traders		Four or less traders		Eight or less traders	
All	31.1	13.3	39.1	19.6	28.5	12.7	36.5	18.2
Old	31.8	13.6	40.1	20.0	29.4	13.0	37.7	18.7
Other	0.0	61.1	0.0	61.1	0.0	61.1	0.0	61.1

By regular reference to the "Commitments of Traders" report, it is possible to keep a quite current notion about how the important segments of the trade feel about price prospects in traded commodities. Oftentimes it is possible to review price action during the reporting period and see clear evidence of changes in market posture on the part of large traders and commercial hedgers.

The effects of small trader actions is usually not so discernible (unless they constitute a very large part of the entire open-interest), and the reporting period contains some price action that bears heavily on their trading interests.

mercial grain dealer, to remain in business, may have to buy supplies in a high-priced cash market, and sell the merchandise a few weeks later in a low-priced cash market—and they do! Only if they have been successful in their hedging activities can such merchandising losses be offset and sustained. Finally, commercial interests (and, to some extent, the producers) tend to be the only market users that enjoy a continuing and clear-cut choice of offsetting their market positions, or making or taking delivery in settlement of matured futures contracts.

In view of all of this, the commercial hedgers must be considered preeminent factors in the marketplace. They are not always right in their judgments, by any means. But they must be right for larger sums than they are wrong, or they would cease to deal in futures contracts at all.

The monthly "Commitments of Traders" report provided by the Commodity Futures Trading Commission is the very best guide we have to the trade's expectations about price movements. Not only does the "Commitments" report break down the *strong hands* and the *weak hands* for us, it also shows us where these groups of traders and hedgers stand at the end of each month. A little time spent analyzing the "Commitments" report in the light of price movements during the 30-day period covered should add tremendously to your feel for trade attitudes—and should greatly reduce the chances of your doing something foolish that can cost money.

To demonstrate the usefulness of this report, we will now take the issue dated August 31, 1984, and go through it with some degree of care. By so doing, the careful trader will be able to see the role this data should play in any well-structured trading program.

By consulting Chart 9–1 we see that reportable positions are broken down to *non-commercial* and *commercial* holdings. These figures become available by virtue of the fact that all market participants must report long and short and spread holdings whenever these commitments reach certain prescribed levels. Although the commercial interests who are engaged in bona fide hedging have no trade position limits on them, as the non-commericals (nonhedgers) do, the commercials still must report their futures positions in accordance with CFTC regulations—or face serious penalties. In view of the reporting requirement, it is possible to do the following monthly market arithmetic on each traded commodity:

	Commercial (hedgers) open-interest	long	short
Add	Noncommercial (nonhedgers) open-interest	long	short
	Totals		

Subtract these category totals from total open-interest to get nonreportable (small trader) long- and short-interest.

In checking open-interest in wheat (Chicago) at the end of August, we see that there was a total of about 233 million bushels of the grain represented in contracts open in all maturities, by all classes of holders. It must be remembered that each contract requires a long and a short; hence, the shorts have open commitments to deliver 233 million bushels of wheat, and the longs are committed to accept 233 million bushels of wheat and pay for it. However, both the longs and shorts may choose to offset before the respective contract maturity dates by making equal-and-opposite transactions in the variously held contract months. Except for 1 percent or 2 percent of the holdings, offset will be chosen in preference to staying around to make or take delivery. Recognition of this fact underscores the reality that both hedgers and speculators—be they large or small—are dealing in the risks of ownership, rather than ownership, of wheat. However, since they are all looking for profits, we can now take these report numbers apart and draw some valuable insights about how they expect to profit from the market positions they have chosen.

The last contract in winter red wheat (the kind traded in Chicago) is July, and it will be seen that practically all of the open-interest is now held in *old* (current crop-year) contracts.

Looking now at "Percent of Open Interest Represented by Each Category Of Traders," we see that at the end of August, commercials (hedgers) held 54 percent of the total long-interest, and 36.6 percent of the total short-interest.

While hedgers consistently point their trading activities to *basis,* or price-differential considerations, here we see that the hedgers are net-longs by a substantial margin. Regardless of how one gets long, and whatever the reasoning behind it, it is an unalterable fact that if prices go down, longs lose money. Being a hedger doesn't alter this, unless the hedger holds equivalent positions long and short. We can see the hedgers' faith in higher prices to come: They prefer the bull side of wheat by some 40 million bushels. Or put another way, the hedgers favor higher prices by a ratio of 3 to 2.

Now let's try to trace this conviction on the hedgers' part and see if their bullish inclinations are strengthening or weakening.

The line that sets forth "Changes in Commitments from July 31, 1984" tells us that the commercial hedgers reduced their short holdings by more than 17 million bushels during the month of August, but they only reduced long holdings by 4 million bushels! The biggest operators in the wheat market favored the long side of the market over the short side by a ratio of 4 to 1 during the month of August.

Let us now turn our attention to the public, nonhedging traders.

The reporting level on wheat is 500,000 bushels. What this means is that anyone—or any firm or interest—that holds 100 futures contracts (a contract being 5,000 bushels) must report this to the CFTC in accordance with pertinent federal regulations. The noncommercials can be viewed as large, individual traders. The CFTC report tells us that at the end of August, this group of 104 big, private speculators held about 7 percent of the total long-interest and almost 14 percent of the short-interest, and that during the reporting period this group reduced its long holdings by some 1.4 million bushels, while increasing its short commitments by 19 million bushels. Conclusion: The large traders were swinging to a clear bearish sentiment during the month of August. In view of their trade posture at the end of the reporting period, it's obvious they were looking for lower prices. The spreading by noncommercials is insignificant. At less than 6 million bushels, we can only assume that basis considerations aren't distorted enough to attract much attention from the speculative trade.

In addition to commercial hedgers and noncommercial large traders, the brokerage houses also come under the reporting requirement. Any time a commission house has aggregate positions of customers on its books that reach 500,000 total bushels in wheat, it must report its holdings to the CFTC. We can consider the category headed "Nonreportable

Positions" as principally comprised of public positions that are being handled through brokers. These are, for ease of consistent identification, the weak hands in the trade mix. Individually, these commission house customers may be farmers, university professors, or taxicab drivers. Some of them may make a full-time business of commodity speculation. Others may trade a few contracts per year. All we can be sure of is that their individual positions are less than 500,000 bushels—or they would be required to report as individuals, in which case we would find their data in the noncommercial category.

It will be remembered that public traders overwhelmingly favor the long side of the markets they trade in. However, this positions report contains a surprise. It shows us that at the end of August the small public traders held almost 46 percent of the total open short-interest, along with 35 percent of the long contracts!

We also see that these traders reduced all of their market commitments during the reported month, but that they closed out more than three times as much short-interest as they did long holdings. Knowing that public traders are always vulnerable to squeeze pressures—especially with the commercial interests solidly aligned on the opposite side of the market—we know what to look for in price/volume data through the period involved: It will be a price run-up accompanied by fairly impressive volume, occasioned by desperate public shorts offsetting under fire! The total result made open-interest fall about 6 percent, as the trade was clearly reluctant to follow the price-move.

Turning now to the wheat charts for August, the full scenario stands revealed: The short-squeeze began at the end of July and ran into August, as the wheat price (December contract) soared 20 cents per bushel in seven sessions.

When the first flurry of departing public shorts subsided, the price promptly fell 9 cents, which put a note of hope back into the hearts of the remaining nervous shorts. But their optimism was short-lived. The sessions of August 7 and 8 brought another upturn that carried to $3.74—and blew a lot more public shorts away, who had been sitting on the edges of their chairs since the last week in July.

With the weak-handed shorts now gone, no one remained who was willing to pay up for December wheat. Prices began falling and continued downward to the end of the month, with intraday trade holding within a 3-to-5-cent range.

Something else is clear from the August data: While daily volume remains a little bouncy—indicating greater than usual sensitivity to higher prices (as nervous public shorts continue to run from each successive scare)—total open-interest is falling in response to the lower price range. Conclusion: The trade is unwilling to follow price lower. Although it would be impossible to get the bears to admit it, from their actions in concert with the bulls, we can see that market concensus supports the idea that prices should be higher!

The astute technician will know that there is a rule to be applied here: When open-interest goes down as price goes down, longs are offsetting. The situation is technically strong.

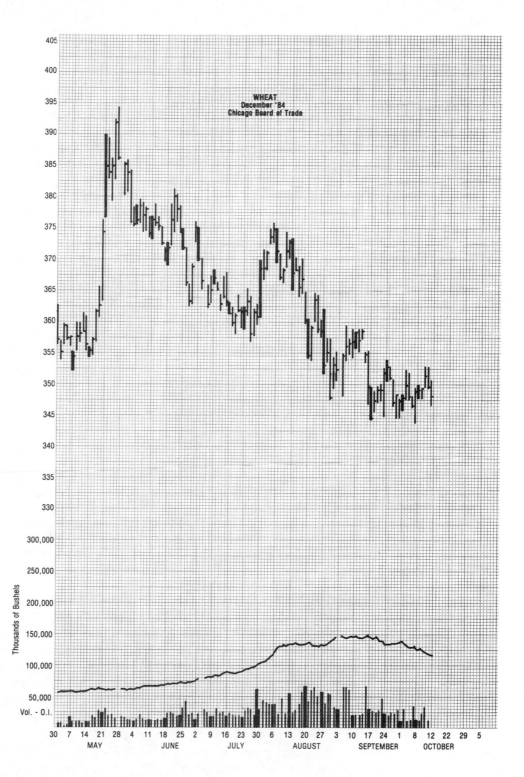

Chart 9-2

This December 1984 wheat contract demonstrates how the traders will follow a trend. In spite of the fact that the longs in this situation were paying for the lower prices, open-interest continues to build steadily from May until August. Not even the 15 cent break in the last two weeks of June and its continuation through July could discourage the bulls. As soon

Chart 9-2 (*concluded*)

as one set of longs were chased out, newcomers took their places—as witness the constant buildup in open-interest.

The spurts of volume that signal a squeeze of some proportions come in connection with higher prices in July, August, and September. Traders who could read the technical signs understood that commercial hedgers were strongly on the long side of this contract through the summer, with the public constituting the majority of the short-interest.

The public traders are usually wrong, but they are not always wrong. This is one of those times!

This is especially true because of the mix we see, with hedgers firmly entrenched on the long side. They will offset when they think it serves their purposes—not in response to a transitory price fluctuation. With such a large contingent of strong hands holding long and with such an unusually large coterie of public traders in short positions, higher prices on wheat futures are to be confidently expected. Even if one is not willing to take a long position and be exposed to the vicissitudes of this widely-swinging price range, there is no way to justify going short in this situation!

The strong-handed commercial hedgers are overwhelmingly bullish.

The weak-handed public traders are the major short contingent.

Open-interest is dropping as prices move lower. The trade isn't following the move downward.

In view of all of this, there are two—and only two—places to be with respect to December wheat futures in mid-September: long, or on the sideline.

Position Report Is Required Reading

Anyone who attempts to trade commodities without the information contained in the monthly CFTC report is simply deluding himself. Obviously we might wish it were more current when it reaches our hands, but even in its tardiness, it provides information and insights that are crucial to speculative success. If one's interest leans to gambling on unknowns, Las Vegas has more to offer than the commodity markets.

It has been underscored that public traders tend to overwhelmingly take the long side of any contracts they trade, but they don't always do so! The August 1984 CFTC report shows you a dramatic exception to their usual pattern of behavior. This bit of information by itself could prove crucial in avoiding trouble, but there is much, much more guidance to be gleaned by the individual who learns how to understand and critically analyze the report data. Doing so calls for an established review procedure.

1. With the CFTC report and the pertinent charts showing daily price, volume, and open-interest before you, make a day-by-day evaluation of changes in these data over the period covered by the report. If you find a significant price drop, accompanied by high trade volume and

a reduction in open-interest, look into the numbers and see it for what it is: offsetting by impaired traders on the long side, profit taking by short-holders, and a general unwillingness on the part of both longs and shorts to follow the price into lower ground. Such a development on the face of it indicates technical strength, but we must look further.

2. For open-interest to shrink, both longs and shorts must offset. We must, therefore, determine whether the longs that left the contract were more likely to be hedgers or speculators. Our clue to hedger response to price change relates to the effect it had on carrying-charge premiums or discounts.

Since we know that on the 1st of August the commercial interests were heavily net long, we must assume they were *long the basis*. This is to say that they owed grain or product deliveries to customers, and need to acquire the actuals in order to meet their contractual obligations. Their long contract purchases, consequently, were undertaken as a means of establishing the forward price at which they will be able to acquire the real grain: either by remaining long and taking delivery from their opposite-side short-sellers, or by swapping futures contracts for cash wheat in ex-pit transactions, or by purchasing cash wheat and simultaneously selling out an equivalent amount of futures contracts.

If the charts disclose an appreciable widening of the basis between cash and futures, or between nearby and more distant futures, then we should be mindful of the probability that the hedgers may be offsetting to cash profits on the long legs of their market position. That hedgers are offsetting is a certainty if the basis premium approaches anything like the full costs (elevation, storage, insurance, and interest charges) of holding the physical commodity over the time period involved. This is so because we know that carrying charge premiums will never exceed this total; a hedger will try to cash his basis profits at the most advantageous level—and reposition his hedge sales in other, perhaps more distant, more promising maturities.

If, on the other hand, the premiums and discounts were little affected by the price runup, then it's reasonable to assume that the strong hands are still well positioned on the long side of the market, waiting for alterations in supply/demand balances or other market inputs to produce the profits they seek.

Using a straightedge, proceed from left to right on the charts, beginning with the last day of the preceding month, at which time the CFTC report tells you how the market holdings mix was made up. Look at each successive day in light of price stimulus and volume/open-interest response, as well as any important alterations in price differentials between the cash and all corresponding contracts.

As the data are progressively revealed, the trader should be able to proceed from the initial market diagnosis of strong, weak, or neutral to appraisals of greater strength, greater weakness, or continuing neutrality.

Every significant price change should be pondered in terms of who it helped and who it hurt. Related changes in trading volume and open-interest should be searched for clues to what the winners and losers did in the face of their new threat or opportunity.

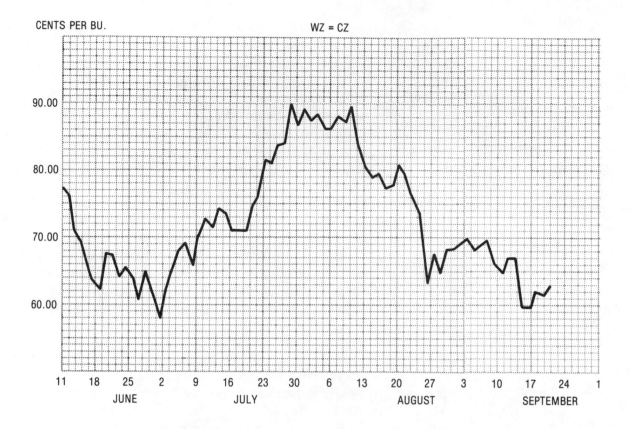

Chart 9-3

This spread chart affords a dramatic demonstration of *substitutability* between wheat and corn. Theoretically a farmer can feed wheat and corn almost interchangeably, except for the consideration of cost. Wheat commands a higher price than corn; however, wheat has a higher nutrient value than corn.

Through this summer period we can see how the premium on wheat went from 77 cents to 58 cents, climbed to 90 cents, and then broke back down to 60 cents. When this bushel of wheat costs only 55 cents more than a bushel of corn, wheat becomes an attractive grain substitute for corn in animal feeds, and in this fashion an oversupply of wheat is consumed at an accellerated rate.

Commercial interests and large public traders are oftentimes trading intercommodity spreads like this one, looking to changes in relative values as a result of shifting balances in supplies and demands for the substitutable products. Since both sides of the spread are December contracts, the only consideration is wheat price versus corn price.

Once the technical trader develops the capability of running across a commodity chart and evaluating the action/reaction sequence that stands revealed in the tracings, he will soon discover that he can—in a fair proportion of cases—draw reliable conclusions about what the trade will do in the face of a projected development. This is the very essence of technical market forecasting and should be the ultimate objective of everyone who uses charts for any purpose whatsoever. Doing this imposes the necessity of being able to look at each event through the eyes of all of those who are involved.

Needless to say, the appraisals a trader makes will not all be correct, but by thinking each market confrontation through, he will add immeasurably to his analytical abilities and alert himself to a spate of possibilities that would, otherwise, go completely unnoticed.

In summary of this topic, several points can be briefly made. First of all, no particular group of traders can be credited with a clear-cut superiority in forecasting the course of flat commodity prices. Commercial hedgers, large speculators, and small public traders all have their roster of successes and failures to protect them against the sin of complacency. To the extent that some make profits while others take losses, the underlying cause is invariably due to better trading practices, rather than vastly superior information.

The reason that a public speculator should carefully appraise the mix of holders on each side of a given situation before committing himself is to obtain the potential protection that is afforded by traveling in powerful company. The commercial hedgers and large speculators have the ability and the willingness to engage in a certain amount of defensive trading. While protecting their own positions, they will also protect the interests of the smaller traders who are in the van.

The reason a prudent speculator should try to avoid associating himself with a market position that is occupied by a preponderance of small public traders is not because they are any more likely to be wrong in their judgment (in a single instance) than their larger counterparts. The weak hands are weak because they perform so very badly in the face of vicissitude. They are always vulnerable to a threat from events or more powerful market forces, and when they begin abandoning a situation, their own desperate efforts to extricate themselves from mounting losses only serve to multiply the problems of all those who happen to be in their camp.

The ideal course, quite logically, is to always try to trade with the strong-hands and always try to trade against the weak hands. The only recurrent exception to this is when fundamental supply/demand considerations are deemed sufficiently strong to outweigh the technical hazards—for example, at the end of a harvest, when seasonal short-hedging begins to taper off, or a surge of seasonal buying by commercial bulls offers the likelihood of giving prices a steep and perhaps protracted buoyancy.

Look at Both Sides of a Position

Most important, and this can not be said too often or too emphatically, try to overcome any inherent tendency to be bullish or bearish. Look at the market with a completely open mind. If prices are headed lower or the small public traders are overwhelmingly holding the long side of a selected contract, you should either be short or on the sidelines. If the fundamentals look even mildly constructive and there is a large public short interest, you should be long or on the sidelines.

But, regardless of all else, the only test of a right position is in the profits it produces. And it is a clear and irrefutable fact that all commodity prices cover the same distance in downtrends as they do in uptrends. If a review of your market activities discloses a lopsided score, as concerns long and short positions held, then it must be conceded that a mental bias to one side or the other is hampering your trading effectiveness—and, quite as likely, costing you money in the process.

Rid yourself of any mental blocks. Don't consider anything except the matters of inherent strength or weakness, based on the fundamentals, and potential strength or vulnerability, based on an analysis of the technical indicators. Then take the position the facts support. When you can do this, you are trading like a professional.

Profits flow to the strong hands in the market, but developing them is more a matter of intellectual conditioning than it is of anything else.

If you can develop the *methods* that produce trading profits, don't give the dollars a thought. They will follow automatically.

10

Understanding the Conflict in Commodity Price Volatility

In order to understand the constantly fluctuating patterns in commodity prices, one must begin with an appreciation for the reasons which prompt market users to take positions.

Basically, of course, everyone who trades commodity futures does so for the purpose of making a profit or avoiding loss. The speculator hopes to make his profit by either:

1. Offsetting a long position at a higher price than his purchase price.
2. Offsetting a short position at a lower price than his selling price.
3. Offsetting a spread position at a wider or narrower price differential, depending on the nature of the dual position he holds in different contract months, different commodities, or different market locations.

Hedgers Seek Protection and Profit

The hedger uses the futures markets as a means of obtaining a sort of variable *profit insurance*. He seeks to minimize loss exposure and, hopefully, show a hedging profit by offsetting his hedges at a more advantageous basis or price differential, as between his cash inventory (or cash commodity sales commitments) and the somewhat equal and opposite position in futures contracts.

In the case of both speculators and hedgers, however, you can be sure that the overwhelming majority of all futures positions will be offset, rather than settled by delivery of actuals. And the time remaining in any given contract before offset (or delivery) is mandatory is always precisely fixed.

The longest possible time a position can be held open is dictated by the trading life of the contract still remaining. In most agricultural commodity contracts the longest period this can ever be is a few days less than one year, assuming that one takes a position on the first trading day and holds it until the last trading day of a selected contract.

In practice, however, the trading time remaining in most positions held by either speculators or hedgers is much less than the life-of-contract maximum. This is true, because both hedgers and speculators demonstrate a consistent preference for the nearer deliveries, rather than the more distant ones. This pattern may be due to the greater volatility of nearby prices, or the greater predictability market users attribute to the shorter time span, or both. But whatever the rationale, that nearby contracts get the lion's share of trade attention is undisputable.

Interest Often Builds Slowly

Chart 10-1 shows a characteristic buildup of open-interest from the first trading day. As time passes, the trade begins to take more notice of the contract, as measured in open-interest. Peak interest in the contract is reached about 90 days before its expiration, after which the open-interest dwindles rapidly, indicative of both long and short holders offsetting their positions—rather than waiting for expiration—and closing out by the making or taking of delivery.

While the open-interest pattern shown in the meal chart may be accurately labeled characteristic, it is by no means the only tracing that can occur. An examination of other charts will show that great surges of open-interest can occur at virtually any point in contract life, depending on the attractions that exist. Since one contract open necessarily involves one long and one short, each holding opposite sides of one contract, open interest can be viewed as a measurement of difference of opinion in the marketplace. To state it another way, before a speculative seller can make his sale, he must find someone who thinks the price offers an attractive purchase. Before a speculative buyer can make a purchase, he must find someone who thinks the price is already high enough. (Similarly opposing views are present in spreads, also, but may not be as clear-cut as in flat-price speculation.)

Conflicting Opinions Must Exist

In view of the ever-present divergence of attitude, as between buyer and seller, open-interest can be considered the best possible quantitative measurement of the opposing interests that have a sufficiently well-developed price idea to prompt them to risk money on their viewpoints. Generally, the larger the opposing forces, the larger the size of the potential battle when they confront each other in the pits and try to make their conflicting viewpoints prevail.

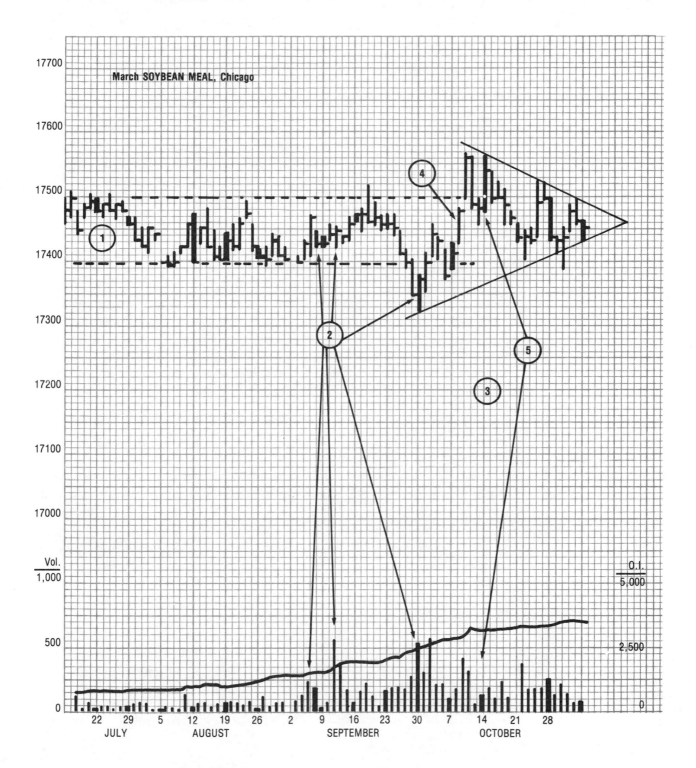

Chart 10-1

The 100-point trading range (1) produced little excitement, as shown in both trading volume and open-interest. However, when the sessions of August 27 and September 3 (2) failed to break through the bottom range level, the shorts must have begun to worry. Volume on both days documents the notion, at least. Lower prices on the 6th and 11th put the pressure on the longs, and it persisted until the reversal on September 30.

Beginning on the reversal day, a buildup in open-interest and a progressively narrowing trading range starts to form the *pennant* that often precedes a major move to another pric-

Chart 10–1 (*concluded*)

ing level. During this period of increasing congestion (3), both longs and shorts reflect a good deal of self-control in adversity. However, when the shorts failed to run from the price action on October 7, 8, 9, in anything like record numbers (4), the longs were clearly under pressure, and a lot of bulls did offset on the 10th, after the attempt to go over the $175.70 level failed.

The run-up on October 14 was absorbed by the shorts (5) on extremely low volume, as open-interest remains constant. But 10 days later, a bulge to $175.37 brought a lot of short-covering on the part of those who suspected the beginning of an uptrend. However, the longs failed to run from lower prices during this pennant buildup, so it was no surprise to see the bull camp finally muster the strength required to make the break-out move to the up-side.

Note that a long holder of this contract would have lost 50 points over the entire charted period. The short would have been an equal amount to the good. In the interim, a single move could have made or lost 200 points.

Watching such a confrontation shape up can at once be enlightening, exciting, and extremely profitable, providing you can accurately pick the force most likely to be victorious and then join its ranks.

Chart 10–1 offers an example of market forces gathering for a major encounter. Over a period of several months, from the opening of trading in this contract, we see prices holding within an unspectacular 100-point range. Trading volume is equally modest, with the average session registering about 150 contracts changing hands. However, we note that beginning early in August, open-interest begins to creep upward. Either new longs and new shorts are taking positions, or existing holders are adding to their existing commitments. Quite likely, the resulting growth in open-interest reflects *both* enlargement of existing positions and the establishment of new ones.

In any case, the battle lines are being drawn: The shorts expect price to fall, and the longs are equally confident that the price on the contract will rise. Time alone can tell which camp has the right price idea.

The Struggle Begins

During the third week of September, we see a price drop of about 100 points, accompanied by an impressive increase in volume. On the 27th of September, when the price fell to $173.50, there was a good bit of long offsetting. However, the contract low stood at $173.40—posted May 29—and the greatest collection of stop-loss orders were still resting below the $173.50 closing.

The session on Monday, September 30, was interesting from several points of view. The opening was not particularly spectacular, but it soon became apparent that the bears were looking for a new contract low and the bulls seemed to lack the courage to present much resistance. The price on the contract drifted lower, with excitement mounting at each step of the way. Suddenly at $173.40, a large commission house began offering to sell the March maturity, and as buying bids edged lower, the sellers showed no inclination to argue with the market offers. There was now no doubt about it: Disappointed longs were giving up. Their stop-losses had been resting just under the old contract low, and they were now being hit.

Volume surged as pit brokers struggled to buy back their customers' losing positions. The bears kept the pressure on for a while, until it became clear that offerings were diminishing. The pit began to quiet down and the possibility of a turnaround became a haunting possibility. Then, slowly at first, a few bids appeared at a few points above the day's low. Pit shorts met the exploratory buying with more selling, and the price was hammered back to the day's low. But more buying came forth, and as it did, it now became painfully clear that a reversal was in the making.

Reversals Come Quickly

The time had now come for the shorts to run for cover. As they shouted and waved their bids for the contracts required for offset, it was the recently hard-pressed longs who were holding out for ever higher prices. The tide had turned completely in the course of a few minutes. Price continued to climb, and the session closed within five points of the day's high.

The action constituted a key reversal, and there were few technicians who failed to realize it. October 1 and 2 were continuations of the uptrend, marked by stronger prices and persisting good volume, as shorts were forced to buy back their impaired positions in a market now dominated by aggressive bulls.

October 8 and 9 offered another demonstration of classical technical behavior. From the new contract-low set on September 30, a lot of chartists anticipated a 50 percent retracement. However, they apparently felt that if price exceeded the half-way mark on the upside reversal, it could portend a continuing bull-trend. As a consequence, a lot of offsetting by shorts was prompted by the penetration of the $175.60 level on the 9th. Other bears rushed in to take their places, though, and this, coupled with eager buying on the part of confident bulls, was reflected in a net gain in open contracts. The session of the 9th gave the bulls a new burst of assurance, but the short contingent met them order for order, and again open-interest inched higher. With such a demonstration of tenacity on the part of the bear camp, it was the bulls' turn to have second thoughts.

October 10 proved to be a session firmly controlled by the shorts. From the opening bell they could sense an opportunity for lower prices. And, while die-hard longs tried to meet the onslaught for a while, it soon became clear that the cause was futile. Lower prices ruled to the final bell, and the day closed near the low.

Disappointments Trigger Surprises

On the 22d we again see trader response to a price chart that exceeds the 50 percent retracement expectation. The bulls had failed to post the new contract high they were shooting for on October 14, which was viewed by many as a dire signal. Then, when the contract broke below $173.50 on the 21st, a rash of offsetting by disheartened longs swelled volume and reduced open-interest. With price continuing lower on the 22d, we again see the surge of volume that suggests flight on the part of damaged or apprehensive traders.

The next key day in the life of this maturity came on November 11, and it can be considered to have broken the last line of bull defenses. September 9 had produced nearly a 100-point jump in price, and volume had blossomed with it. Now the bulls had every reason to believe, if a new contract high could be made, there should be quite a harvest of short offsetting in the new price ground. The only discouraging evidence appeared in the open-interest graph. Neither higher nor lower prices seemed to elicit much change in total trader commitments. The best that could be said for this indicator was that it appeared to be about holding its own.

November 11th produced the new high price the bulls were seeking, but the bears seemed to pay no attention to it. Not only did volume fail to increase, it actually dropped slightly below the preceding Friday's level. The message was now clear: The weak hands were largely gone from the short side of this contract. Those that remained were prepared to stick to their guns, and, unless some new development demanded a vastly revised opinion, the probable course of price was *lower*. This is because, as the chart action so patently shows, strong hands were manning the battlements on the short side of the contract.

From November 11th until the contract expired, it was a long succession of bad news for the bulls. Three abortive rallies were mounted at various times, but they could never go far. In fact, volume data that combined with price action in the rallies strongly suggested that the bulges were largely the result of weak-handed shorts offsetting in the face of some small adversities. If these nervous holders had shown the courage of their convictions to anything like the extent demonstrated on November 11th, the price down-trend would likely have been much steeper and longer than it turned out to be.

The purpose in recounting these events in such detail is to demonstrate how the technician in the market must be able to reconstruct the actions that give rise to various kinds of evidence and also how each turn of events is a more or less direct product of interacting conditions that grow out of trade responses to threats and/or opportunities.

Expect Action/Reaction Sequence

A successful commodity speculator must always view market behavior as a succession of actions and reactions. The events beginning in November, which have been recited above, were initially set in motion by a relatively unimpressive increase in soybean meal usage. But this factor could, by no means, be deemed sufficient to precipitate the full course of events. The consumption figure only served as the fuse on a highly ex-

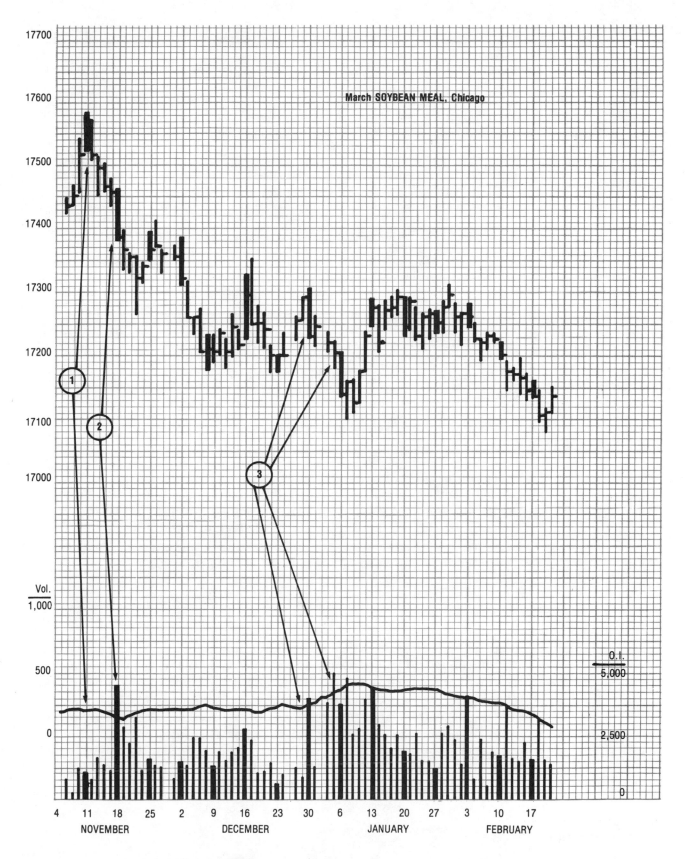

Chart 10-2

The much-looked-forward-to contract high price that was posted on November 11 (1) was a disappointment to the bears, certainly, but it was even more devastating for the bulls. When the new high was posted *without* setting off a wave of short-covering, it might be said that the silence was deafening. Now the longs had to live with the lonely knowledge that

Chart 10–2 (*concluded*)

their old shorts had left, and in their places were a new bunch who had sold higher, or were well represented in the contingent known as strong hands. In any case, they seemed to be highly squeeze-resistant.

A 60-point drop on November 18 (2) served to show how the discouraged longs felt about their chances. As the price fell through the $174.00 level, and three days later broke $173.00, *both* shorts and longs were offsetting.

From the 19th of November until the day following Christmas, little of consequence transpired. Then we see a steep build-up (3) in open-interest, big volume, and sharply lower prices. It looks like the start of something big, but the technical steam had gone out of the situation, and the calendar was running out, also.

After the new year's dip, price returned to the old trading range and then followed open-interest downward toward expiration.

---

plosive situation, and one, it should be repeated, that had been building for several months.

Let us now examine the factors that played important parts in the drama.

Big Open-Interest

Most importantly, the open-interest was quite large. Both commercial hedgers and speculators were deeply involved in the contract. As long as price remained within the relatively modest bounds that the chart reflects until the end of September, both hedgers and speculators were content to wait on developments. In the interim, the size of the powder charge continued to grow, as measured in open-interest.

Bunched Resting Orders

The second most important consideration related to *resting orders*. Public longs had placed stop-loss orders closely below the long-standing trading range. If the price fell below that level, they were willing to take their small losses. But they were not willing to hold on for a big loss.

By the same token, cautious shorts had placed their stop-buy orders slightly above the top of the well-recognized trading range. Additionally, there is no doubt that a lot of traders had orders resting with which to establish new, or add to existing, positions—either long or short—should prices move out of the trading range in either direction.

Most Opening Gaps Are Filled

Now let's look again at the opening on October 9, which was 20 points higher than the previous session's close. A bullish rumor was the stimulus for this price jump. However, as is usually the case, day traders and scalpers in the pit sold the higher opening short.

If the opening had been lower than the preceding close, they would likely have been buyers on the opening bell. The reasoning is that the price gap between one day's close and the following day's opening will probably be filled in, thereby affording short-term traders an opportunity to take a small profit on an exceedingly quick trading turn. Gaps between closes and openings are commonplace, but the gaps that remain at the end of each succeeding session are really quite rare.

The higher opening also attracted the attention of strong-handed commercial hedgers, who saw the better price level as a good opportunity to sell some short hedges. But there were even more bullish interests on the opening. Buying pressures outweighed offerings with the result that, after the first few minutes, the price was forced constantly higher.

Traders Change Opinions

Mid-session selling developed, but it was unequal to the task of halting the price rise. As soon as the selling orders had been filled, the upside move resumed. It was at this point that a lot of bulls began to suspect they were seeing something that was far more substantial than a mere "technical correction." These new converts became highly aggressive buyers, establishing new positions or adding to current commitments at the top of the trading range. Open-interest data shows us that for every short that departed, another appeared to take his place, since in spite of the squeeze the shorts were experiencing, trader commitments in the contract held about unchanged.

The tip-off to the bulls should have been in the October 9 volume. Such urgency to do something in the face of rapidly rising or falling price is usually related to losses, rather than opportunity. Routine buyers or sellers are able to be far more deliberate than any brand of loss-motivated offsetter. In the absence of an increase in open-interest, such a volume spurt in the face of sharply higher price should have been highly suspect, even though some news seems to give it a measure of fundamental validity.

Of course, the latecomers that bought high on October 9 were the same folks who sold low the very next day. There is nothing more to be avoided than buying at the top of a short squeeze, unless it is selling the low end of a long squeeze!

The Battle Never Stops

The confrontation between buyers and sellers is unceasing. The only things that change are the balance of power between bullish and bearish interests, and the willingness of new traders to join one camp or the other. As the foregoing material should have demonstrated, success in moving price lower or higher may convey an immediate benefit while setting the stage for even greater reverses a short distance down the road.

For example, the bulls may successfully raid the shorts in a contract, but, once the weak-handed shorts have been chased in, lower prices are in excellent prospect.

All of this should serve to underscore the verity that commodity trading tends to be a series of short-term engagements. You may occasionally hear a broker or trader discuss long-term commitments in connection with a commodity position, but they are extremely rare. When they do exist, they are far more likely to involve spreading than flat-price speculation.

If the opportunity for a long-term tax trade presents itself, by all means take advantage of it. Any good broker will be able to tell you how to hedge the paper profits and wait out the remaining time. But don't waste time or effort trying to preselect such situations. If they come, be grateful. Whether they come or not, trade for the best profit at the smallest risk. In this way your tax bill may be higher, but so will your bank balance.

It's impossible to go broke taking profits, regardless of how big the tax bite may be.

11

Study the Action to Forecast the Reaction

We have already underscored the verity that price is a thoroughly undependable basis for making a trading decision, unless it can be considered along with other information over a period of time, or in light of comparisons with prices of other—somewhat similar or marginally substitutable—commodities or products.

The most we can ever hope to confidently state about the fundamental underpinnings of the price of anything in a relatively free, moving market is that:

1. The price appears to be in an acceptable relationship when compared to historical price/values, to the prices of other products in other locations, and over varying time intervals with respect to delivery.
2. The price appears to represent an *under-valuation* when appraised in light of the considerations set forth in (1), above.
3. The price appears to represent an *over-valuation* when appraised in light of the considerations set forth in (1), above.

Price as an Effect

These quite simple sounding dicta contain the totality of so-called fundamental price/value decision making. In talking of market fundamentals, we must look at price as a *rationing function,* based on the market's appraisal of supply/demand balance. In other words, the *fundamental-*

ist looks at price as being an effect of changing balances between supplies and demands, and the market's variable ability and willingness to buy the product and consume it.

Price as a Cause

Conversely, the *technician* in the market tends to look at price as a cause, rather than an effect. He also sees price as a constantly fluctuating continuum, but he knows that a given price action will exert an absolutely predictable economic effect on a known group of position holders. The one thing he does not know (for a certainty) is what the response of the affected position holders will be. But, even here, excellent criteria are contained in the changes in open-interest and volume, which are regularly summoned forth by changes in price.

Just as any price might be the right price for a commodity at a given point in time, any trade volume and any open-interest level might be encountered in a selected futures contract, with no obvious significance attributable to it, except in terms of comparisons with other contracts or with other time periods in the life of the contract being examined.

Technical trading—or chart trading, as most practitioners identify it—is a practice in evaluating the significance of changes in relationships, as measured by price, trading volume, open-interest, and the relative mix of strong and weak hands on either side of the positions held open in a single commodity contract. These individual indexes are widely variable, subject to sudden shifts, and largely devoid of anything that might be accepted as a characteristic configuration in an average market. As a consequence, the chart trader is constantly engaged in evaluating the composite changes in the indicators and, from these appraisals, maintaining a sort of continuing progress report on the contracts in which he has an interest.

In order to lay another foundation stone for the student's introduction to technical market analysis, we will deal at some length with a May soybean oil contract.

In the interests of clearer explanations, we will also presume insights into the interests and behaviorisms of the position holders, which are never quite so transparent in the world of reality. Our purpose in following this demonstrative methodology is to let the reader see the relationships between certain actions and reactions, then to apply this empirical information to other situations in the market in an effort to improve trading performance and profitability.

The contract opened at about $8\frac{1}{3}$ cents per pound, and at the end of the first 90 days, this May oil had traded in a range of from 832 to 720. We can also observe that volume tends to pick up briskly along with each plunge in price. Noting this effect brings us to an important technical trading rule:

> Rule: When trading volume goes up, and price goes down, new selling pressure is evident. Either the longs are offsetting, or new selling is in the market—or both.

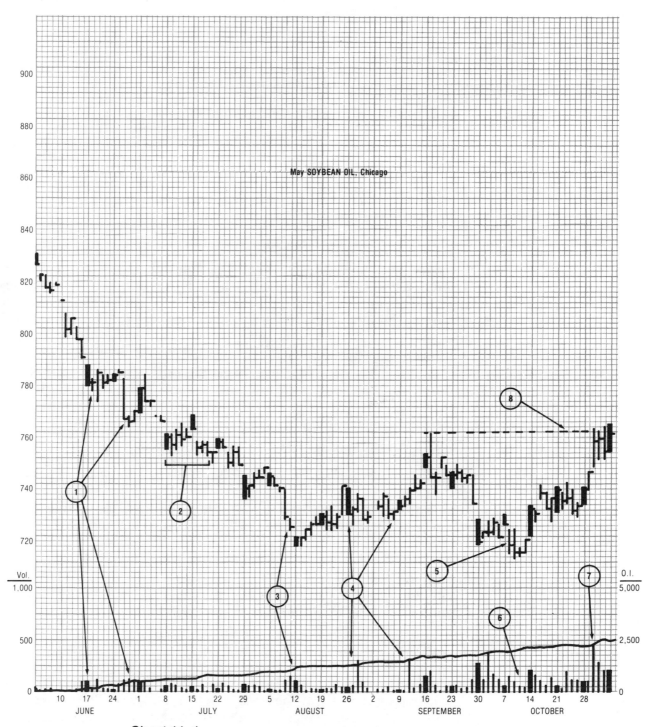

May SOYBEAN OIL, Chicago

Chart 11–1

Hopeful bulls repeatedly looked for the bottom in this oil contract, but each plunge into new low ground (1) forced a rash of offsetting. The little bulge and a three-week plateau built bullish hopes (2) that were dashed on the 20-point break (3) of August 7, 8, 12. During this entire period, upside moves tended to shrink volume and flatten open-interest; the trade wanted no part of larger holdings at higher price—and the bears were much too confident to be chased in on a modest upside fluctuation.

Mid-August to mid-September (4) is a period of marking time, except for a couple of short-squeezes, when price moved fractionally over old resistance points in the chart. (cont.)

Chart 11-1 (*concluded*)

Open-interest during this period might, in the clear view of hindsight, appear to be looking bullish, but until the jump in open-holdings on September 12 and 13 on higher price—and the drop on the 17th and 18th on lower price—there was nothing in this indicator to signal a growing bullish sentiment.

It was when the new lows of October 8 and 9 (5) failed to produce big volume (6) that the bottom seemed assured. Open-interest resumes an upward course (7), and it is the surges into higher price ground that brings volume responses—as weak shorts leave under impairment, and eager bulls press the drive.

The break into new interim high ground on October 30 (8) was crucial in forming this well-defined *W*—or double-bottom. Although the figure's architecture is a little sloppy on the second leg, it was enough to buoy bullish spirits who were eagerly seeking reasons for higher prices in a quite confused fundamental situation.

Since we can see that open-interest continues to climb perceptibly, we must deduce that even if some longs are run out on these price dips, other buyers are taking their places at the lower levels. If longs were offsetting in the face of the squeeze and shorts were taking profits on the dips, the result would be a reduction of the total open-interest. But since this is not happening—in fact, quite the contrary—we can only conclude that for three months the market is technically signaling a lower price level.

> Rule: When trading volume goes down, as price goes up, there is reduced buying pressure. A downside reaction is likely.

We see the requirements of this rule being met throughout August and September. The price bulges fail to trigger either much in the way of short offsetting or new long buying. We are therefore able to conclude that the trade was unwilling to follow prices into higher ground, and each bulge was met with a prompt dip back into the lower range. All of the classical signs of a one-way bear market were inherent in this chart through the end of September.

A Change of Heart Shows Up

During the first two weeks of October, however, we see a clear change of persuasion on the part of the traders in this contract. The return to the 720 level on September 30 had produced a good deal of volume, logically viewed as tired longs offsetting in the face of still another disappointment. But when successive contract lows were posted on October 8 and 9, volume just dried up! All of the longs had run that intended to do so. Those that remained (and open-interest shows us that there were a lot of them) were getting ready to take the initiative away from the bears, who had had everything their way for over four months.

The shorts held on bravely from 720 to 750, but when the price hit 765 on October 30, it represented a four-month interim high and set off an avalanche of resting stop-buy orders. It was all over for the bears at this point, and the triple signal left little doubt about what was to come:

> Rule: When prices go up, accompanied by an increase in trading volume and an increase in open-interest, the situation is quite bullish and may indicate the beginning of a major upside move.

We can see that all of the requirements of these strength indicators are met. We note that price, volume and open-interest do, indeed, all increase together. Moreover, after the upside short squeeze has run its course and (on November 1) price turns downward, volume dries up, and open-interest doesn't appear to have been much affected at all.

Analysis: The willingness of traders to follow prices higher is evident; but they seem strangely reluctant to press the short side of the situation. Higher prices are a near certainty!

At the end of October, May soybean oil has an open-interest of 2,500 contracts. The mix of commercial interests, large speculators, and small public speculators is roughly the same on both the long and short sides of the contracts held open. Daily volume averages about 500 contracts being traded, and open-interest appears to be growing at a rate of about 50 contracts per session.

The Bulls Control

The situation for a bullishly inclined trader appears most attractive. To begin with, there is sufficient open-interest and daily trade volume to provide a good trading climate. A high degree of liquidity exists in the contract, as proven by the fact that average daily volume approaches 8 percent of the total open-interest. This high level of trade is handled without reflecting the wide swinging price aberrations that are the hallmark of a thinly traded contract—of the sort that all except the most steely-eyed professional should studiously avoid.

The excellent ratio of daily volume to open-interest (within a quite modest daily price range) lets us know that this contract is being well served by pit scalpers, who usually stand ready to sell at a small fraction above the last sale or buy at a small fraction below the last purchase. (In commodity markets, scalpers perform essentially the same function carried out by specialists on the securities exchanges. But instead of being assigned to the role, as the stock specialists are, the pit scalper is merely trading for his own account, seeking small profits on a very large volume of transactions during each session.)

Turn now to Chart 11–2, and observe the price and volume bars on December 11 and 16. On the 11th, this contract opened 10 points higher (3) than the previous close, made a new life-of-contract high at 847, and then closed at 842. Price action of this kind can bring forth all manner of interpretation from various segments of the chart-reading fraternity. To

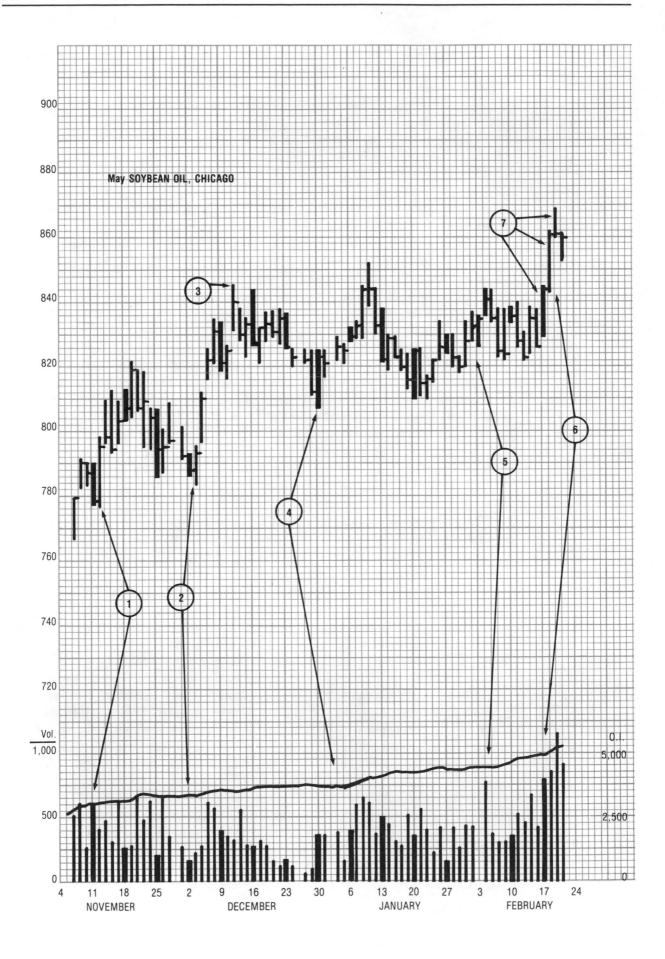

May SOYBEAN OIL, CHICAGO

Chart 11-2

The first four months of its life, May oil displayed all of the classic signs of a bear market. Then followed a period of three or four weeks in which traders formed a whole new opinion about the situation.

It is now the shorts who display their nervousness by running on each upside surge, as measured in volume and open- interest (1 and 2). Sharp setbacks take out a collection of weak-handed longs occasionally, but the average volume of trade in periods of lower prices is much smaller (as in the last two weeks of December). It is when a move up comes that we see the shorts are in trouble (4), and volume tells us what they are doing about it. Open-interest assures us that new sellers are taking the departing losers places, so we can assume that the bull move is still intact at the end of December. One of the most reassuring signs for the bulls is that the short squeeze (3) on the 11th fails to produce either the volume or reduction in open-interest that indicates a trustworthy reversal.

Once the two weeks of indecision in early February had passed (5), the building open-interest and the shrinking volume on the dips are validated in a sharp run-up (6) to a new life-of-contract high (7).

In view of the big volume accompanying sharply higher prices on the 17th, 18th, and 19th of February, a turnaround seemed at least an excellent possibility. The contract immediately sold off to about 820 and expired at about 845.

---

some, it will be seen as a warning to the bulls. To others, it will be read as a harbinger of an upside move. To still others, it will have no real significance at all, since the intra-day high failed to produce big volume, and the closing price was not below the previous day's close.

Regardless of all this, the careful technician will go well beyond the matter of price open, high, low, and close in his attempt to forecast the probable next phase in this contract. Most important, the new contract high price failed to spark big volume. The shorts refused to stampede, and, of equal moment as concerns the probable shape of things to come, open-interest fell hardly at all.

Analyzing the Symptoms

Now let's run some of these events through our all-knowing crystal ball and find out what really happened, since all that these numbers amount to are symptoms for the market doctor to analyze and then diagnose.

Certainly, much of any volume that grows out of higher prices has to be considered as primarily occasioned by weak shorts, all liquidating at about the same time. Stop-loss buying started the price bulge on December 11, and it wasn't halted until a new contract high was made, probably taking out all but those foolhardy types who hold positions without protective stops and others who understood the fluctuative risk well enough to place their stop-buy protection somewhat above the precise tick required for a new-high on the contract. But the biggest enigma in this is that open-interest barely wavered.

We have a technical trading rule that tells us:

> Rule: When open-interest goes down, as price goes down, disappointed longs are offsetting, and this is an indication of technical strength.

And there is yet another:

Rule: When open-interest goes up, as price goes up, new buying is present. The bulls are in command.

To merely look at the daily price bar, it is clear that price did, indeed rise: The close on December 11 is some 15 points higher than the intrasession high of the preceding session. But open-interest doesn't appear to have dropped enough to merit notice. So, just how should a session of this kind be looked at?

Understanding a Turnaround

In a sentence, any session that produces anything that might be considered a turnaround should be looked at as two distinct entities: without doubt, you're dealing with an *action* and a *reaction*. It pays to be able to recognize and analyze them. The professional traders, especially pit scalpers, who make a lucrative business of buying price dips and selling price bulges understand the action/reaction sequence, and capitalize on it. Although the public trader must steer clear of the small dips and bulges, since the higher nonmember commission rates she pays make trading minor fluctuations too costly for the profit opportunities they offer, the larger dips and bulges do offer reasonable profit opportunities on relatively short trading turns. On this basis they deserve to be understood and considered as speculative possibilities by both the full-time and part-time trader.

It has already been pointed out that a higher opening than the preceding close will usually elicit selling on the part of pit traders. Also, if the price on a designated contract opens below the preceding close, pit traders tend to be buyers at the lower opening. For the trader who sells the higher opening, the probability is that the price will work lower, affording her an opportunity to buy in her short position at some small profit. In the opposite circumstance, the pit professional buys the lower opening, expecting the price gap to be filled—and enabling her to sell out her long contracts for a quick, if small, profit.

Although only a small minority of the floor traders who regularly follow the above procedure are able to explain the technical rationale that makes it work to their advantage in the majority of cases, there are two technical trading rules that apply very nicely:

1. When open-interest goes down, and price goes up, disappointed shorts are offsetting, indicating technical weakness.
2. When open-interest goes down, as price goes down, disappointed longs are offsetting, indicating technical strength.

While there is no way of absolutely proving the minute-by-minute effect on open-interest that is occasioned by a higher (or lower) opening (such detailed market information is not available on a continuing basis), it is among the safest of assumptions that the first effect will be a reduction of open contracts through offset.

In the case of a higher opening, public traders who hold short positions may be stopped out if the opening is substantially above the earlier close. In other cases, public traders who are watching the tape may be merely scared off by the price jump and choose to liquidate their short holdings, rather than take their chances at the questionable mercy of a market that in the first few seconds of trade already seems to be a most menacing affair.

Strong Hands May Also Run

Opposite these weak-handed shorts who are being chased out of their positions by the higher price are strong-handed public traders and pit professionals who see the higher price as an invitation to sell. To whatever extent the strong hands hold open long positions when the opening bell sounds, their selling to the liquidating shorts must result in a reduction of open-interest. If price opens higher and then continues to climb higher still, the buying pressure of offsetting, frightened shorts—and presumably aggressive selling by the professionals, well-financed public traders, and commercial hedgers—may dramatically reduce open-interest. In any case, once the shorts have been chased in, there will not likely be sufficient new buying pressure to sustain the price rise.

At this point, trading volume can be expected to slacken. Bids to buy will contain more deliberation than loss-charged urgency, and the price will begin trending lower to fill the gap created by the higher opening.

In the case of a lower opening, the foregoing can be recited virtually word for word, except in the opposite context. On a lower opening, it is the weak-handed longs who are under fire. And since the small public trader overwhelmingly favors the long side of any market, his flight in the face of price adversity may be even more precipitate, because in a long-shake-out, there will usually be more of the weak-handed small public traders.

But the other factors are about the same. The lower opening will attract outside professional and pit buying, which will sop up the offerings of the liquidating longs—and reduce open-interest in the process. Once the disadvantaged longs have sold out their impaired positions, offers to sell will dwindle, trading volume will taper off, and the situation is technically set for the reaction, which will usually be a higher price level and complete or partial filling of the price gap that triggered the sequence initially.

From the foregoing, then, we can only conclude that while the longs always want higher prices, it is the eager offset-selling of despairing longs that make fluctuative lows in price patterns. On the other hand, while the short-holders always want price to move lower, it is their rush to buy in impaired or deteriorating positions that puts the fillip on the top of a price bulge.

Both the weak-handed long and short tend to be quite choosy about the price at which they take on a new position. But, when trouble arrives in the form of adverse price change, they care little for eighths, quarters, or even cents per trading unit. All they really want is **OUT**! And they often pay a much dearer price than is absolutely necessary for the privilege of a speedy offset.

By becoming a better market technician, you will be able to enter positions more advantageously. But even more important perhaps, you will be able to study the action, look ahead to the probable reaction, and while removing yourself from the stampeding herd of liquidating position holders, actually capitalize on the trading opportunities their mindless (but quite predictable) behavior affords.

The gapped opening on December 11, followed by a new contract high, certainly took out a lot of weak-handed shorts. But open-interest held quite level. During the next two sessions, as price trended lower, the trade remained modest, and volume kept shrinking as the price backed down to 807. An analysis of the action/reaction sequence traced out in volume responses to price movement tells us that the bulls still retained a discernible edge insofar as courage and conviction were concerned. However, December and February reflected a two-sided market, and 820 to 850 stood as a perfectly obvious trading range that identified the market's revised idea about the right price for May oil.

Look behind the Surface Evidence

Market data, of necessity, only reflects composite totals at the end of each trading day. But each alteration that takes place, as compared with the preceding session or any other pertinent period of time, should give the perceptive technician a greater or lesser piece of trade behavior information to ponder. Of course, there is no guarantee that a certain pattern of response will be continued, but *persistence* in prices and trader reactions is one of the most often repeated behaviorisms we have to work with.

Until something dramatic happens to signal the beginning of a new phase, count on any kind of trend continuing. You will be right in the majority of cases.

12

Sellers Make Great Buyers— and Vice Versa

People have a great penchant for attaching labels to things, including people, and this practice has had the effect of endlessly deluding a lot of trusting souls who accept the labels at face value. This is especially true in the market, where attitudes and price ideas often change at a rate to make a chameleon red, blue, or green with envy.

It is true that a bear in market parlance is always a seller. Likewise, a bull is always a buyer. But even the most devout bear must, at some point, become a bull, because he must otherwise make delivery. Such a course of action would have to be considered most unusual. This is merely to say that the overwhelming odds are that anyone who sells short will, at some point, buy back his short contracts in order to offset—and thereby avoid having to become involved in handling the physical commodity through the market's delivery procedure.

The same thing is true of the bulls. Unless they eventually become bears and sell out their long holdings prior to contract expiration, they will have to take delivery. Few of even the most enthusiastic bulls are inclined to accept the actuals in settlement.

The above-stated facts are borne out in statistics that show that only about 2 percent of all commodity futures contracts are settled by delivery. Ninety-eight percent of all open contracts are settled by offset—which proves that sellers almost always must be buyers and buyers must almost always be sellers some time prior to contract expiration.

Since we know that for every open contract there must be a long holder on one side and a short holder on the other, we have a completely reliable guide to built-in supply and demand in the contract being analyzed. We also know that, since short positions exactly equal long positions, it is theoretically feasible for all open positions in the contract to be offset and closed out at any time during the contract life.

Perfect Long / Short Balance

Granting all of this, the question then arises, "What causes price fluctuation?" With both a buyer and a seller required to open each contract position, on each side for as long as the position remains open, a perfect equilibrium situation would seem to prevail from the outset. Also, since a contract can be offset whenever any former buyer and any former seller choose to execute an equal and opposite transaction, this also appears to connote a fine continuing balance of market forces.

In spite of all this, future prices do fluctuate—widely, at times. And the short-range changes that take place may have only slight, if any, relationship to the so-called fundamental considerations of supply and demand. It is not unusual to see prices moving contrary to the direction in which clear and firm fundamental information says they should move. The serious student of futures markets may find a lifetime of study insufficient to fully explain such perversity. But a few dicta exist to guide him.

The price/value of every traded commodity is a continuum of fluctuations, up and down, great or small, with major moves usually reflecting changes in present or projected supplies and demand. But—to reiterate for deserved emphasis—supply and demand considerations are not the only elements involved in price-making decisions. Short-term futures prices, especially, respond constantly to what must be identified as trader psychology. A fractional-cent change in the price of wheat futures is not likely to be identifiable with tiny change in the supply/demand equilibrium surrounding the grain. Even the most sophisticated economic measurements are incapable of making such microscopic analyses.

Every Trade a Compromise

Small price fluctuations above or below an identifiable equilibrium level can, at most, be viewed as an indication of relative compromise, as between buyers and sellers at the moment at which a given price is posted. Obviously, sellers always want the highest price, and buyers always seek the lowest price. Every transaction, therefore, must represent a compromise of greater or lesser degree on the part of one or both of the traders involved. When the price moves higher, it does so because the sellers are pressing their case successfully and the buyers are giving ground by paying up for the merchandise. When prices move lower, it is due to the relatively greater strength of the buyers, who are insisting on a better (lower) price—and the sellers feel constrained to yield to some degree.

Now, to return to the thought which began this section: *all holders of long positions are potential sellers.*

For the same reasons, *every holder of a short futures position is a potential buyer.* The exceptions are too rare to spend time on at this point.

Look for the Trouble Spots

The essential consideration in technical analysis and forecasting in a futures market is attempting to determine the points of strength or vulnerability at which we might logically expect offsetting to result in

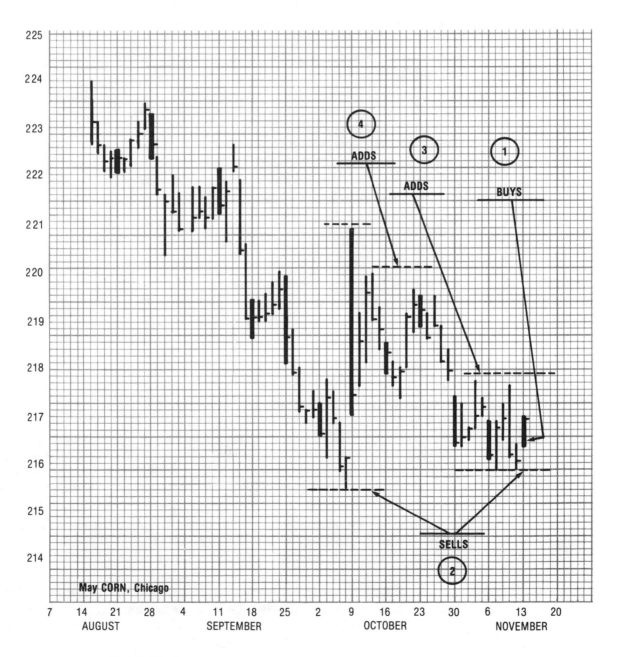

Chart 12-1

heavy buying or heavy selling, largely precipitated by adverse price movement.

Looking at Chart 12–1 through the eyes of a long-holder who buys on November 13, at 2.17¼, we might say that if he pays any attention to chart patterns, he will see 2.16½ and 2.18½ as crucial points in days to come. The admonition to cut losses short and let profits run might suggest that he would place a stop-loss-to-sell order at about 2.16⅜. If the price goes below 2.16⅛, it will represent a new contract low and might be expected to trigger a substantial amount of stop-loss selling, as well as some additional selling pressure by bears who would take the opportunity to add to their short lines.

Conversely, 2.18½ might look like a good place for the long-holder to add to his line. By the same token, if the price reaches this level, the shorts might very likely see this as a good place to get out, rather than stay around for a possible squeeze and the risk of larger losses that could result.

There is always a possibility, of course, that the speculator—whose psychology we are attempting to probe—will arbitrarily decide that when he has picked up a given number of dollars in profit, he will close out. Should this be the course he pursues, we will have no very good clues as to where he bows out.

But we can determine where he will be in trouble, and trouble moves markets infinitely farther and faster than routine profit taking. Traders tend to cash paper profits in quite an orderly fashion, but it is the stampede from losses in front of a price rise or fall that really provides market fireworks!

Anatomy of a Squeeze

Viewed in the perspective of a sequence of events, the classical long- or short-squeeze—with an attendant major price move down or up—is the product of several inputs. First of all, for the phenomenon to exist, there must be sufficient open-interest to provide the required backlog of potential stop-loss buying, or stop-loss selling, when the crucial price level is reached. Second, the weak hands and the strong hands should be well divided, essentially occupying opposite sides of the market. Third, a lot of stop-loss orders should be resting at levels sufficiently close to permit one cluster of stop-orders to carry the price to the next level of stops, etc. When this situation does exist, the effect is a kind of chain reaction, not likely to be quelled until the great majority of the weak-handed holders have bought in or sold out their positions and have been replaced by new holders at the higher or lower price level (or the contracts have been taken by opposite position holders who elect to offset and take their profits).

Needless to say, the weak hands are always more vulnerable to squeezing than the strong hands. It is also axiomatic to point out again that the weak side of the market overwhelmingly tends to be the side favored by the small, undercapitalized, overextended, poorly informed, and easily frightened public trader. This is what makes it weak. It takes little to create panic among such an aggregation, and when it has begun, their flight is not likely to be halted until the exodus has run its total course.

Defensive Trading

Provided the weak hands and the strong hands are somewhat evenly mixed and occupying both sides of the market, a price rise that threatens the shorts will oftentimes be met with aggressive new selling. The effect, predictably enough, will often be to contain and drive back the bull move. In the opposite frame of reference, a slide in price that endangers the longs may bring forth waves of strong-handed buying, thereby protecting the price from penetrating what is deemed to be a crucial level. The effect is often identified as an area of *congestion* in the chart.

However, defensive buying or defensive selling is an exercise that must be left to those who have both the impressive finances and the unflappable nervous structure to wage financial warfare. Such an effort that fails to accomplish its purpose is certain to have only worsened the situation when the blow does fall. It is not belaboring the point to say that defensive trading on the part of a small public speculator is worse than futile. It's madness! Unless you are prepared to sell 100,000 bushels of wheat at each half cent or quarter cent up, or buy like amounts at similar intervals down, don't attempt to prop a market. It will break you!

The public trader should, therefore, always try to be on the side of the market favored by the strong hands and be aligned against the weak holders. To the extent that he succeeds in picking this advantageous posture, he can depend on his strong-handed company to defend his interests when such activity shows hope of being successful. And additionally, he can count on his powerful allies to press hard when an opportunity appears to put pressure on the opposing camp. He may not always be a winner, but the probabilities of profit are strongly in his favor.

To sum up here, data exists to guide any trader in his selection of the most promising commodities, contract months, and market posture as concerns taking a long position, a short position or no position. But mere availability of the information accomplishes nothing, unless the potential beneficiary is willing to spend the required time in familiarizing himself with the tools and learning how to use them.

Everyone is not equally motivated. As a consequence, it seems safe to assume that there will continue to be enough hip-shooters in the market to provide the reservoir of losers that, of necessity, finance price movement.

It is equally safe to point out that anyone who approaches speculation with a scholar's attitude is beginning with a huge advantage over most of his public competition. Study usually brings expertise, and in the market it's spelled *m-o-n-e-y!*

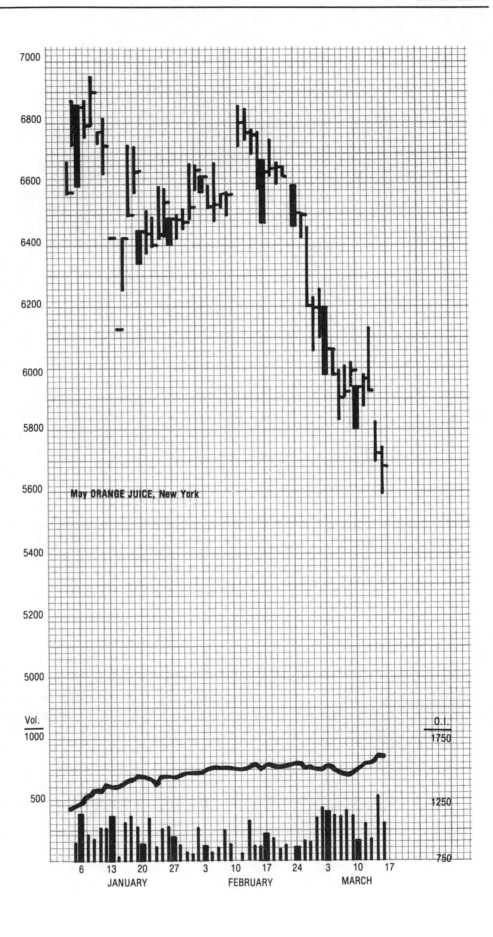

May ORANGE JUICE, New York

Chart 12–2

This chart reflecting two and one-half months in the hectic life of May 1969 orange juice deserves to be framed and hung on the wall of every public trader. It shows a situation in which virtually all of the long-holders were public traders, and practically all of the short-holders were hedgers or spreaders. Or, to put it another way, the weak hands were the longs, and the strong hands were the shorts.

If proof is needed, take a straightedge and check price action against volume and open-interest changes on a daily basis. Note that while price was trending higher through the last week of January and most of February, the shorts seemingly ignored their flat-price losses. This is due to the fact that hedgers and spreaders are trading in price differentials. The *can* ignore a flat price, as long as their position basis performs satisfactorily.

But now observe the volume response to lower prices! The public longs stoically bore the brunt of a five-week break that covered some 1,250 points and took $1,875 off the value of each contract held open. And please note that during most of the period, open interest was holding steady or increasing! As fast as some losers were chased out, other bulls stepped in to take the "wrong" side of the contract.

So long as there are losers enough left to finance a price trend, there is no technical reason for a reversal. But when the supply of losers is exhausted, prices will reverse—if only briefly—regardless of the fundamentals.

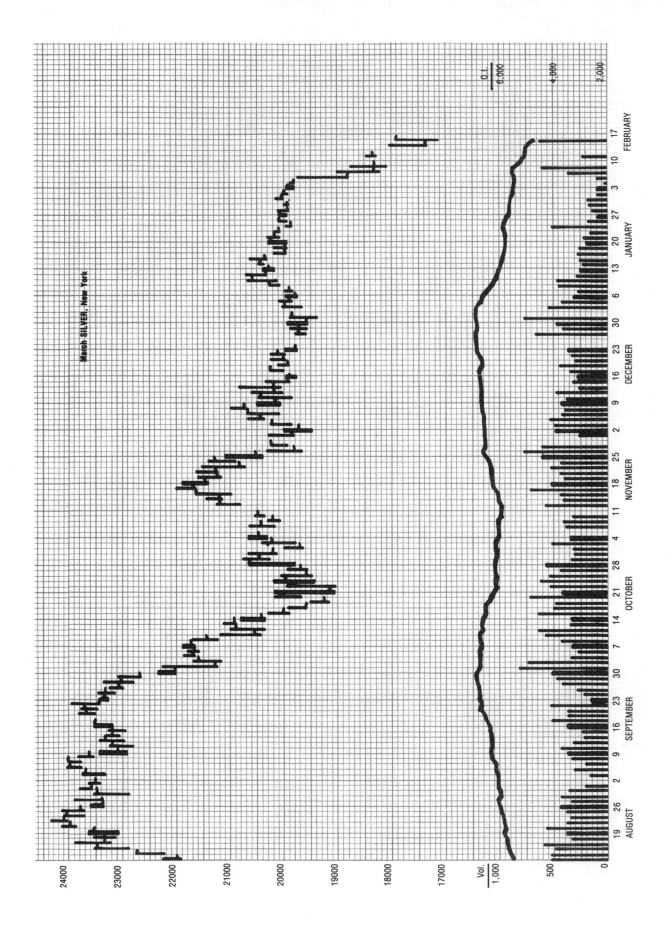

March SILVER, New York

Chart 12-3

The indicators can tell you a good deal about this market that is not likely to be printed in the newspapers. First, by checking relative response to price changes, we can see that the weak hands are holding the long side of the contract. Lower price regularly brings a burst of volume that says, "Longs offsetting." This is not so when higher prices develop. The price bulges quite consistently result in lower volume and (after the end of September) some shrinkage in open-interest. But there is little tendency for the shorts to stampede in front of a price rise, which strongly suggests that they may be preponderantly commercial hedgers (attempting to protect values in inventories) or straddle speculators, trading in price differentials rather than flat price.

Dealing in a situation of this sort calls for steady nerves and a fine appreciation for technical balances. The only sensible course of action is to trade with the fundamentals one can discern, and trade against the weak-handed public bulls. In this case, it's plain to see that such a course would require being on the short side—or on the sidelines, with no position whatsoever.

Joining such an aggregation of poorly performing longs can worry a trader to death, even if one does succeed in taking a profit in the process!

13

Strengths and Weaknesses of Chart Trading

If the reader has gleaned nothing more from these pages than some appreciation and a measure of respect for combinations of charted data that constitute danger signals, the benefits from his new perspective should be extremely valuable. However, if he has also acquired some insight into how technical and fundamental factors can be combined in the positive search for better initial positions and greater profits overall, then the full purpose of this volume has been accomplished.

Too many otherwise effective traders ignore technical considerations until disaster strikes. Then they begin digging in the technical area to attempt to uncover the reasons behind the sudden price reversal that is operating against them. If they are able to find some technical justification for the unexpected event, then they are prone to view the difficulty as one that is likely to be of brief duration and probably of limited significance and price impact. In short, the unsophisticated trader tends to seize on technical symptoms as a good excuse to hold on to a bad position, but he rarely uses the same tools to protect against reversals or to identify new opportunities.

Hindsight always enjoys 20/20 vision.

Technical price reversals are often of short duration, but they are *not always* quickly dissipated. *A long-term trend is just a short-term move that persists.* And persistence in prices is the most notable characteristic we can identify, by the use of charts or otherwise. Stated another way, price that is increasing tends to increase; price that is deteriorating tends to continue to move lower; and price that holds to a horizontal channel tends to continue on a horizontal plane. Minor or modest fluctuations are constant and normal in any free-moving market. However, a two-cent impairment in the price of a bushel of grain— will still cost the trader $200 if he holds two contracts of the commodity concerned. While the fluctuation can perhaps be labeled transitory and modest, its effect on the trader's bank account can be both lasting and appreciable.

Apply Technical Data Positively

If a speculator uses technical knowledge only as an excuse to hold tight to otherwise untenable market positions, he will only succeed in enlarging his losses. As anyone who has traded in the market has learned (probably to his sorrow), an imaginative technician can explain almost anything away on the basis of a *technical correction*. And the term is overwhelmingly employed as a means of rationalizing a loss.

The astute market technician knows there is no substitute for a comprehensive view. He looks mainly to his charts for clues to the short-term strength or weakness in a selected situation, but he also keeps a wary eye on the fundamental considerations that will underpin the longer-term price movements that bring monumental profits or can produce shattering losses.

Being aware of the technical side of the market should vastly improve the choice of initial positions taken. By buying a market that shows fundamental strength over the medium term and technical strength in the short term, the trader has minimized the possibilities of having to sweat out a paper loss before beginning to accumulate profits. Conversely, by selling both fundamental and technical weakness, the best possible opportunity exists for prices to move lower, both immediately and thereafter.

Stay Out of the Traps

Some of the saddest stories to be heard in the markets concern price-chart traders who bought into uptrends or sold into downtrends and who succeeded in getting directly into the jaws of a technical correction. Immediate loss in such a situation often prompts equally immediate offset, after which the unfortunate victims must suffer the frustration of seeing prices move in the direction they had expected all along. When an event of this kind occurs, the traders can be right in the longer term but wrong in the short term—and the short-term error costs him money. So-called bull traps and bear traps are invariably sprung on those who are willing to trade on the basis of a new high price, or a new low price, taking price as the only indicator required. When the trap is sprung, they feel their chart has served them falsely.

Review of a great many such traps discloses that, in all but a handful of instances, short-sellers were caught by soaring price, by failing to heed the message of a new low accompanied by decreasing open-interest. The opposite is also true. We have only been able to find a very few bull traps that were not clearly signaled before hand by declining open-interest at the higher price level.

Dramatic price movement and impressive changes in trade volume are the standard bait that lures unwary traders into such disasters. Seized by the excitement and fearful that they will miss the move, they rush headlong into the trap, invariably acquiring their new holdings from more astute traders who see the danger flags flying and who are either moving to the sidelines or completely reversing their market posture. When the strong hands change their minds and depart, trouble usually awaits those who remain or replace them. Price alone will not tell you when this is happening, but changes in open-interest and the trade mix will. And while each instance may not be clearly revealed in available indicators, when a serious question exists about the proper market diagnosis, **steer clear of it**.

It's at least probable that the average public trader would improve his profitability more by shunning one quarter of the positions he takes than by any other single means. The adventurous spirit is much admired in many areas of human involvement, but it can cause oceans of grief in commodity speculation.

Never be satisfied with what looks like an even break in the quest for a profitable trade.

Unless you can identify what appears to be a distinctly uneven advantage for yourself, stay on the sidelines. **Do nothing** to increase your risk exposure unless you are convinced that you are trading from strength and against weakness. If this sounds less than sporting, then let it be admitted.

Good Sports Die Broke

Speculation is not a sporting form; it's a business and should be pursued solely and exclusively for the purpose of profit. Risk selection is the most important key to success, and this means that there will be many times—even most of the time—when the best position is no position whatever!

Another area in which the technical market follower can find a wide assortment of travail is in the matter of trade timing. As prices move higher, or lower, and open-interest shrinks in company with a lackluster trade volume, all of the signs are pointing to a reversal. Clearly, the trade is reluctant to follow the market. When this happens, a turnaround is the most probable expectation. However, predicting the event may be far easier than putting it on a timetable. And for optimal benefit, the trader should be equal to the task of developing some kind of notion about both the nature of the probable reaction and the time it is likely to occur.

By being too late, part or all of the move can be missed. By being too early, intervening changes in supplies (or fundamental statistics of any kind) may serve to eclipse the technical situation to such an extent that the expected development is not permitted to come to pass. Or, what's worse, new fundamental information may send prices flying in exactly the opposite direction.

Crop reports are notoriously dangerous threats to all manner of traders, for example. Regardless of the impressive architecture of a *double-top* or even the classic contours of a *head and shoulders*, the market is primarily concerned with supply and demand. When this relationship changes, the market will deal first with the new facts, and even the most impressive chart formation will evaporate in the face of a new price-idea consensus.

There Are No Sure Things

Never expect absolute reliability from any technical indicator, or any combination of them. The greatest accuracy of the indicators is in markets where the traders show every sign of understanding the overall picture, and there is little in the way of news or rumor to spark a new surge of enthusiasm on either side of the contract. At a time like this, dull trade and a seeming loss of speculator interest may camouflage the building of a veritable powder keg. Slowly climbing or falling prices may be accompanied by subtle changes in open-interest that tell the technician that someone is getting into trouble. The trade mix of holders will often provide the identity of the vulnerable camp. But even this knowledge is not sufficient in itself. The trader must also know how to gauge the sensitivity of the situation in terms of its susceptibility to being set off, and changes in trade volume is his best measurement of this facet of the market.

Markets Sleep—Traders Don't

It is a certainty that the holders of speculative positions in the sleeping contract are not, themselves, asleep. No one realizes better than they that markets that sleep the soundest also wake up the liveliest. The more the issue narrows, as measured by upper and lower margins of the trading range, the more concentrated will be the attention of those who hold open positions in it. When price penetrates—higher or lower—into new ground, the stage is set for a greater or lesser struggle.

But in order for the market battle to be fought purely on the basis of strong hands versus weak hands, neither side can have important assistance in the form of fundamental changes or new market information. And without such help, the strong hands are the odds-on favorites to win out.

However, if the weak hands happen to be aligned on the side favored by new facts, such a coalition may be able to carry the day against almost any kind of opposition.

It is for these reasons that the best technical trading opportunities are usually found in periods during which little new information is expected. Once the market has learned a fact, it discounts it into future price—and it will never be a factor for change in price again. When most (or all) available information has been so discounted, the only remaining market influence of any consequence is technical in nature. And, given a free track upon which to run, unaffected by any significant influences of a fundamental nature, the technical predictability of a market is greatest. It is also at such times that the potentials for technical price movements must be considered to be widest.

So, while the usefulness and reliability of combined technical indicators are amazingly good, it should not be amiss to again underscore the fact that they are not infallible. Even the most meticulously developed technical case can be upset by a flood or a strike or an unexpected announcement on the part of government. Technical analysis is not a full-functioning substitute for continuing appraisals of the changing balance between supply and demand. In the short term, technical considerations will often stand as the most important influences on price. But over longer periods of time, the stern realities of production and consumption, or inventories and disappearance, take precedence over all else.

Use All the Analytical Methods

Use technical analysis as just one more highly valuable tool in the quest for market profits. While carefully applying the tests and measurements contained in this volume, never for a moment ignore the other categories of information that constantly bear on the problems of trading. If both the fundamental and the technical conditions of a given market are taken into account, it goes without saying that the hazards of loss will be greatly reduced, and the speculative batting average as measured in profits will be dramatically increased.

Not everyone will benefit equally from increased knowledge about the technical workings of the markets. The reason is that traders—like other folks—tend to be a mite lazy. Successful speculation, like any other professional engagement, imposes a tough standard of performance on those who strive for excellence. There is not substitute for careful study and painstaking application of the principles involved. Even while admitting to the clear validity of this truism, there are still altogether too many traders who lack the industry and self-discipline required to produce the success they hope and pray for.

Without seeming to unduly question the possibilities of direct assistance from Lady Luck or Divine Providence, it should be remembered that even God is supposed to prefer helping those who help themselves.

Speculators are not exceptions to the rule.

14

Pros and Cons of Price Patterns

It would be unthinkable to end a volume of this kind without making some comments concerning the strange and, at times, wonderfully captivating patterns that appear in price charts. For those who possess the detective's interest and the scholar's ability to delve deeply into statistical behavior, there is perhaps no field of economic inquiry that offers a more challenging collection of riddles. Multiply such an engrossing intellectual exercise by the promise of unlimited wealth that awaits anyone who learns to perceive the messages in chart configurations, and you have a lure that must be almost irresistible to investigator and speculator alike.

As indicated elsewhere in this work, your author has been deeply involved in a wide range of study projects that sought to develop hard answers to the enigmatic patterns that march across graph paper, as if being drawn by the biblical "finger" that wrote for the ancient prophet. Recounting the long series of project protocols would be of little value, inasmuch as most of the work had to be labeled "not definitive" in terms of results.

There is a feeling of some considerable chagrin, as well as disappointment, in such an admission. At the very least, it would be rewarding to be able to irrefutably show one's peers that the *random walk* theory—so steadfactly urged by some—is as devoid of substance as the pentamerous price syndrome put forth by others. But, before a thesis can be expounded, its product must be consistently definable. Until a firm and unequivocal batting average can be assigned, everyone who speaks to the mooted subject is talking empirics—regardless of his podium.

This author, like untold market students before him, began his probings into price behavior from the seemingly familiar ground of chart-figure analysis. A lot of years, several calculators, and five computers later, it seems perfectly clear that there is more than an involved accident underpinning the appearance of a double-top, double-bottom, island, gap, pennant, flag, or reversal in a price chart. But, like the radionic emanations from deep space, knowing they are there is still a far cry from knowing what they mean.

Perhaps they mean different things at different times, or in company with different conditions. In any case, analysts will continue to pick at the puzzle until someone solves it, positively or negatively. And the solution will be the real prize, not its results as measured in money or merchandise. People solve problems for the same reason that Hillary climbed his mountain: because they are there.

In the course of the work that provided the skeleton structure for this book, several things came to the surface repeatedly as concerns price patterns. They are briefly offered as results—with neither a case in rebuttal nor support. However, when a phenomenon repeats itself with sufficient regularity as to transcend the parameters of statistical probability, then it deserves to be looked at in a different light, regardless of whether or not the investigator can demonstrate a causal relationship. In some cases, the author has a mixture of suspicion and/or opinion about inputs that underlie the effects. But for now, let the effects stand by themselves:

1. *Price trends are not statistical accidents.* Whether in bull or bear markets, *trendiness* is far and away the most distinctive characteristic to be found in price plottings. The best price model (for identifying trend) is, in our judgment, a composite constructed by adding cash price and all current-crop-year futures prices together and dividing by the number of elements in the model. It is demonstrably preferable to use market prices at a predetermined midsession point (e.g., 12 noon) than the more readily available closing figures. Opening and closing prices show great deviation from statistical composites, based on prices taken at other times of the trading day.

2. *Islands are meaningless in thin markets.* Islands in price patterns signify a period of reappraisal in well-traded markets. As such, they deserve trader attention. However, in contracts that reflect small open-interest, the island phenomenon appears to be more a product of poor liquidity than a changing price idea on the part of the trade. In our studies of large markets, price reversals of 10 percent or more of the preceding move followed clear-cut island formations in more than 60 percent of instances observed.

3. *Gaps tend to repeat in both directions.* While the dramatic aberrations in price/value appraisals that create chart gaps equal to 25 percent

of the permissible daily trading limit are rare (less than 4 percent of our sample), when they do occur they overwhelmingly tend to repeat on both sides of the price-movement track. Incidence of price gapping demonstrates a correlative relationship to the trade volume/open-interest ratio in a given contract: The higher trade volume goes as a percentage of open-interest, the more likely price gaps become. Moreover, if a gap occurs on the upside (or downside) in more than two thirds of sampled instances, it is singly or multiply repeated in the opposite direction in succeeding days.

4. *Head and Shoulders defy definition.* This tracing proved too subjective to appraise. Depending on the persuasions of individual investigators, a pattern that meets the definition of one may not meet the requirements of another. Before a phenomenon can be evaluated, it must be susceptible to clear-cut identification.

5. *Double-Tops and Double-Bottoms usually hold.* These patterns mark the effective termination of a given price trend in more than half of the instances examined. However, there is a distinct reliability factor inherent in the time period involved between establishing the two *V*s. An *M* or a *W* that is traced out in two or three sessions is not to be trusted. By the same token, reliability diminishes if too much time elapses between the implantation of each apex.

6. *Pennants point to upcoming explosions.* Well-developed pennants often precede wide-swinging price moves, but their usefulness as price-direction predictors is unimpressive. The congestion that will provide a launching pad for a major price-idea revision is often reflected in a pennantlike chart tracing. However, the shape of the chart figure discloses no more than random correlation to the matter of price direction next following.

Some of the most exciting work this writer has ever encountered in the area of price-pattern analysis was done by the late Ted Holland, Jr. Mr. Holland combined the resources of an inventive mind, a professional background in statistics and economics, experience as a broker and trader, and years of function in the knotty area of market analysis. While his explanation of price behavior as time-series events in a four-dimensional "playing space" leaves much to be questioned, his *price event particle* concept is, to say the least, intriguing.

Aside from explanations, however, Holland was one of the few price-movement analysts who traded for his own account—on the same information and projections he furnished his clients. This fact in itself put him in a class apart from nontrading advisers. It takes no particular skill to invite a client to risk *his* money on any sort of trading hypothesis. But when one's *own* funds are committed, it's a different kind of challenge. Ted Holland traded, and he did the analytical task with little apparent interest in anything except price-chart behavior. There are a lot of traders around who can still attest to the usefulness of the man's advice and can prove their point in the profits realized by following it.

Price-Only Analysis Has Great Weaknesses

It is essentially due to the effectiveness of Holland and a small handful of other commodity-price technicians (who also trade) that your author is unwilling to flatly dismiss the price-only approach to technical analysis as illusory. We will say, however, that it is most difficult to understand how such a methodology can be reliable, inasmuch as it consistently defies statistical proof. Replication of results is the mandatory first step on the way to identification of a science. Unless independent investigators can apply similar tests and obtain comparable results, the procedure must be—at best—considered an art. And this is so regardless of how skilled some of its practitioners become.

The rules and signals that are offered the reader in this work demonstrate a degree of repeatability that deserves the most careful scrutiny of serious traders. At the point where we cease trying to analyze markets and begin analyzing traders, consistent patterns of behavior begin emerging. It is difficult to abandon the orthodox view of price as a function (or effect) of supply and demand, but not until we cast price in the role of the stimulus (or cause) do regularities of response on the part of the market (traders) begin to come into focus.

Trade Makes Market Prices

Price must necessarily be viewed as the economic measurement of supply/demand balance, but for the market technician, we submit that its greatest significance is in the domino effect it triggers in the course of its fluctuations. The market pragmatist has little room in which to argue against the hypothesis that, while supply/demand equilibrium dictates economic price/value, the trading interests (buyers, sellers, nonbuyers and nonsellers) create the effective market price. Since reality never quite succeeds in attaining the perfect market's perfect dissemination of total information, traders must always make their decisions from an uneven amalgam of hard facts and wispy conjecture—in short, in the market that exists!

The econometrist may measure the price/value of a commodity with microscopic accuracy but, unless someone will buy or sell at the declared right price, its practical usefulness is nil. Conversely, any voluntary transaction at any price does accomplish transference of goods or risks of ownership. This comes much closer to meeting the functional role of the market than does the mere establishment of unwavering validity in assigned theoretical value measurements.

If speculators could buy and sell futures contracts in the exclusive frame of reference of changing supply/demand balances, the fundamentalists who understand price elasticity theory and projective techniques would own the market in short order. But it doesn't work this way. The market may not be human, but is users are—and they render human judgments. Knowledge, ignorance, fear, sagacity, charity, and greed are all part of the complex equation that is spelled out in the form of market price. The human animal is a creature of emotion and excesses, and nowhere is this better documented than in the markets. Such aberrations deserve to be held in check, and increasingly they will be.

By shining some light on areas of overreaction, we might expect that other—more level-headed—elements in the trade will take the position of counterbalances, when hysteria threatens to eclipse judgment. If so, there may be a time when we will no longer be able to say, "Whatever the trade does, it *over*does!"

If that day ever comes, the "right price" of the economist and the market price of the trader will still stand apart, but the difference should be narrower than before.

The six charts that follow have been selected to give you an opportunity to apply the information you have gained from reading this book. As you turn to each successive chart, cover the explanatory caption and using a straightedge, make your own appraisal of the trading scenario depicted. Then read the caption and see how closely your appraisals agree.

Two of the six charts reflect only price information. Inclusion of these is for the purpose of letting you draw your own conclusions about the relative dependability of trade decisions based on price alone, as compared with judgments derived from a composite view of price, trade-volume, and open-interest.

Good trading!

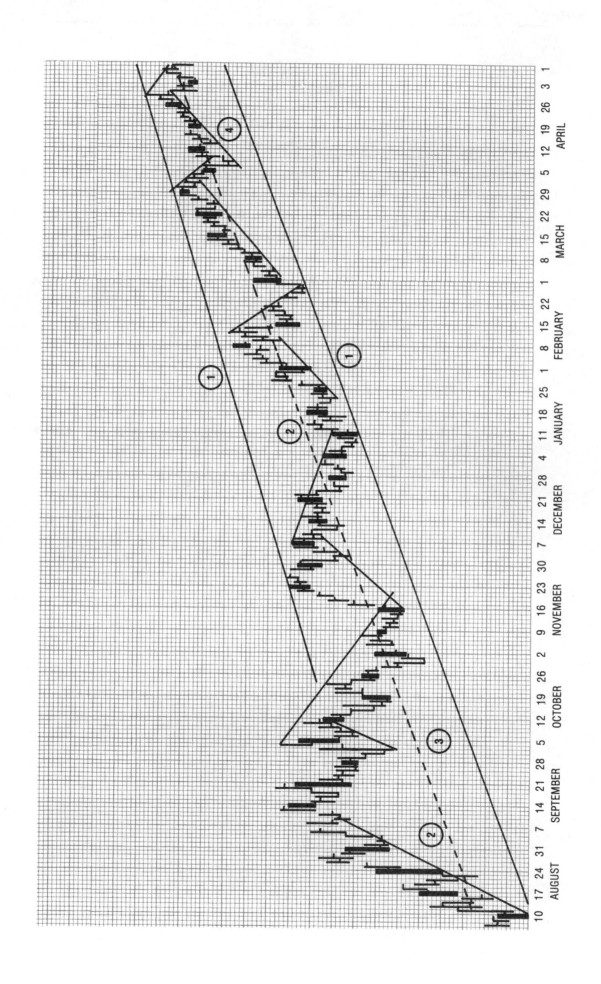

Chart 14–1

The fact that commodity prices do move higher and lower in highly visible directional trends is apparent to anyone who looks at a chart. However, there are several schools of thought as to what produces the trendiness.

This May corn sustained an almost constant march to higher price ground for a period of nearly 10 months. Of course, such a move can only be prompted by a major tightening in the fundamentals of supply and demand. Still, the question comes, "How could price repeatedly move sharply in the wrong direction, as dictated by fundamentals?" (1). The answer lies in the area of informational quality:

A perfectly informed market would, in theory, follow the broken line (2) from the lower to the higher level. Instead, it traded in a range of from five cents in September and October (3), to three cents in March and April (4). And we see 10 distinct periods during which the trade overbought or oversold the contract, based on the trend average. Each time, however, technical corrections halted the move away from the realities, and price came back into midchannel.

This chart should serve to document the fact that there are often a succession of short-term trends and countertrends within the longer perspective of a crop-year or a multiyear production cycle.

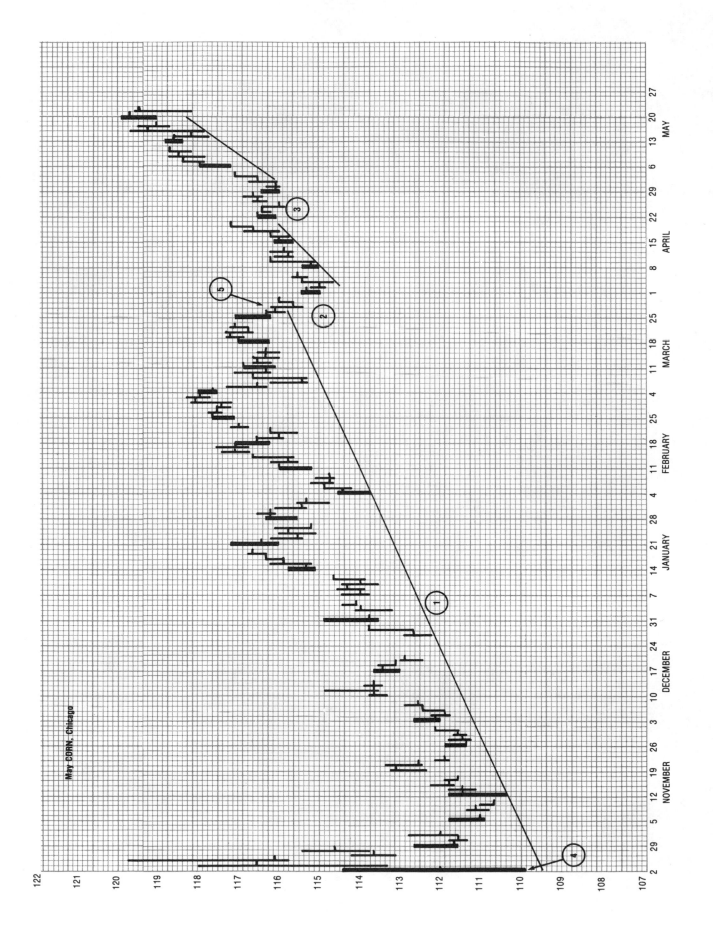

Chart 14-2

Anyone who fancied himself a gap technician could have had the time of his life in the 1963 May corn contract. The only thing that seems obvious is the seven-month uptrend (1), if one can overlook two glaring false signals (2 and 3).

The truly amazing thing about a market of this kind is that there are some devotees of economic Russian roulette who seriously attempt to trade it with only daily high-low-close to guide them. Of course, some of them make money. But even the biggest winners in such a confused situation can hardly attribute the result to trading skill.

This chart offers a great exercise in drawing figures on the basis of price tracings. Among other things, it displays a pennant that covers the period from October 22 (4) until March 26 (5).

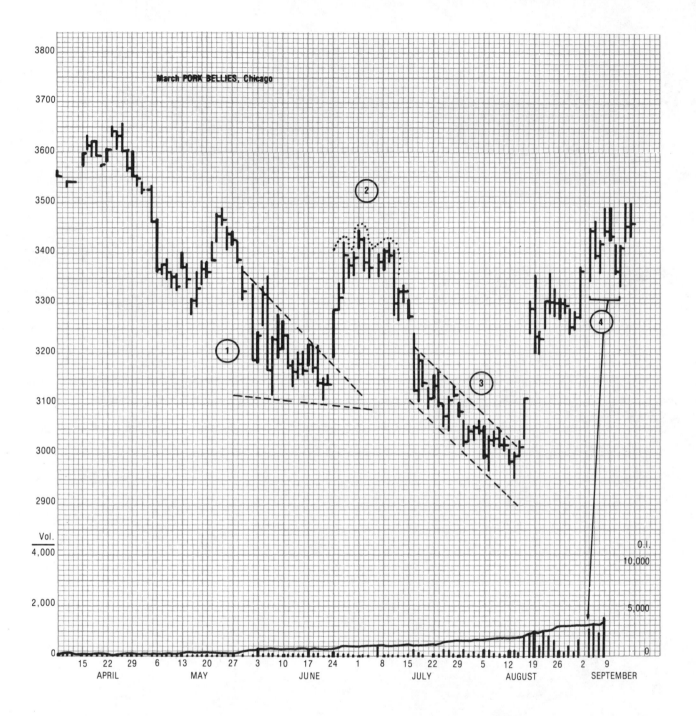

March PORK BELLIES, Chicago

Chart 14-3

This chart covering the first five months of the trading life of March pork bellies is included for the purpose of demonstrating the superiority of hindsight in the analysis of price patterns.

Figure 1 outlines a quite plausible pennant. Moreover, it is tapered downward, suggesting an upside breakout (according to most price-chart analysts). However, the appearance of this figure elicited no trader attention, as we see from volume and open-interest.

Figure 2 is a small, but quite coherent, head and shoulders, and it was followed by an impressive price slide. But again, the trade clearly overlooked it.

Figure 3 is a perfectly believable drooping flag, which, most analysts tell us, is a precursor of higher prices. And the upside breakout comes, but most of the trade missed half or more of the two-day jump.

Figure 4 shows price, volume, and open-interest all climbing together. While the setback of the 4th and 5th was not surprising following such a rise, lower volume and firm open-interest tells us to not worry about it. So, while price continues to fluctuate, the trend remains intact, and higher levels are indicated.

The object lesson of this chart should be obvious. All of the indicators are far more reliable than any one of them. Also, it's easy to find a pattern after it's gone, but to make a profit on it, it has to shed light on events still to come!

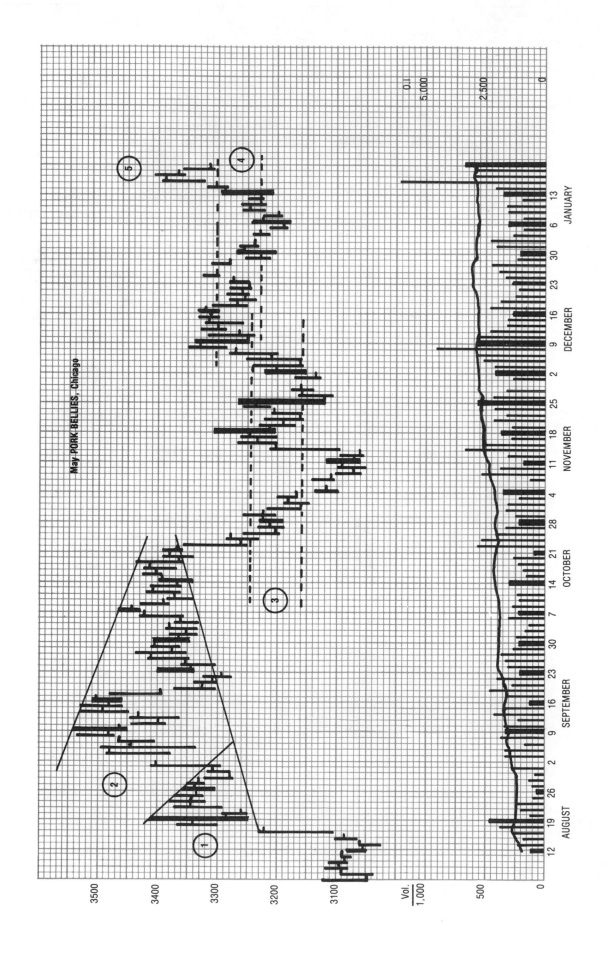

May PORK BELLIES, Chicago

Chart 14-4

This May belly chart offers excellent evidence for pennants, in combination with volume and open-interest. It begins by reflecting all three indicators going uphill together during the week of August 12.

Eight inside-range days form the pennant (1) that breaks into new higher ground on the 30th. As pennant (2) begins to take shape, volume responses clearly give the strong-hands edge to the bears. Note how much wider the trading ranges are on downdays than they are on updays. Also, check the volume responses to the price dips of September 3, 4, 12, and 18.

By mid-October, open-interest shows a tendency of the trade to follow lower prices. The break of October 22 stopped short of the 3250 gap level, but from the volume of long offsetting it triggered, the pennant breakout must have been the crucial consideration to a lot of chartists.

(3) represents the first revised price-idea ranges, which held until early December, after which a slight adjustment upward come on the wings of a short squeeze. The second range (4) was maintained until the longs refused to run in front of the dip below 3200 on January 6.

When the longs refused to budge, the shorts were in technical trouble, which arrived on January 13, carried nearly 200 points higher in four sessions, and produced the squeeze of the 15th. With the weak bears now gone, price quickly returned to the previously established range.

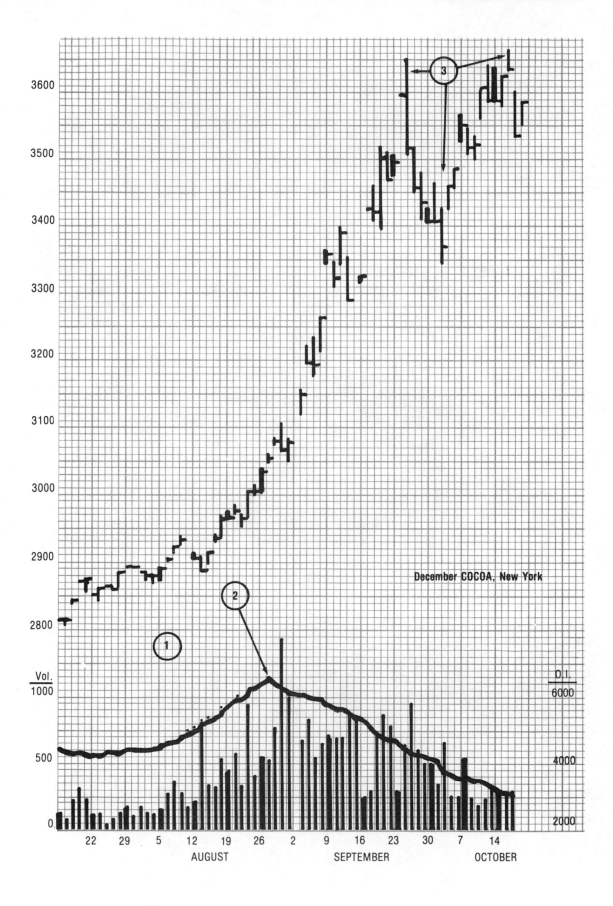

December COCOA, New York

Chart 14-5

Traders in December 1968 cocoa were treated to the spectacle of watching a great change of heart take place very suddenly, but not before the coming event had been clearly signaled.

From early July until late August (1), price, volume, and open-interest were all in agreement about the bull move that was taking place. The difference of opinion between the bulls and the bears was growing at an impressive quantitative rate.

Then, suddenly, on August 27 (2), both camps started to lean to the notion that prices were getting too high. The shorts wanted out, and the longs began letting them buy back their open commitments. We know what happened from the open-interest pattern: Had the longs held firm, the old shorts would have had to make their offset trades with new sellers—in which case, open interest would have held constant. But since interest shrinks, we know the shorts are taking losses, and the longs are cashing profits—all the way to the top!

It is worthwhile noting that in a liquidation phase, open interest will shrink, regardless of what price and volume does. This kind of unwinding phenomenon takes place at the terminal end of each expiring contract, since neither longs nor shorts are interested in delivery.

Note the blowoff on September 25 (3) and the technical setback, followed by another spurt to a new high.

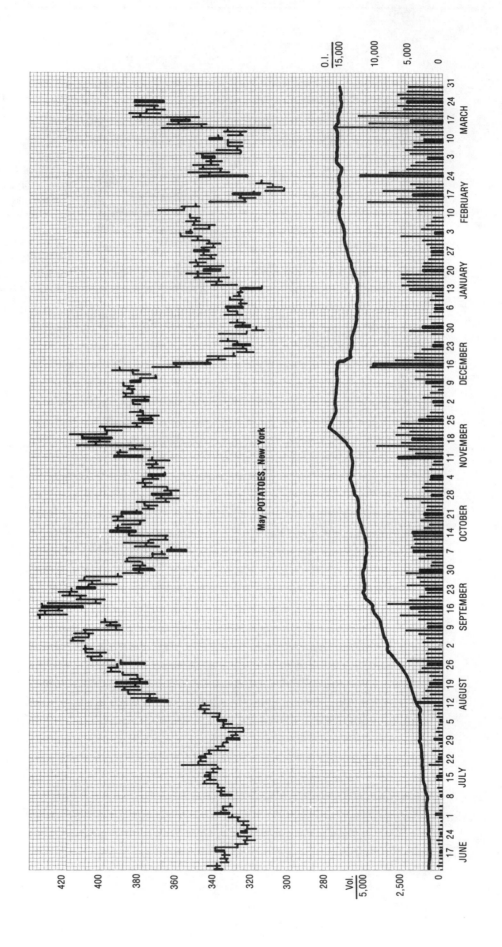

May POTATOES, New York

Chart 14-6

This May potato chart is such a dramatic demonstration of the analytical concepts put forth in this volume, that—rather than set down the sequence of events that produced the results—we invite you to do your own appraisal.

Ideally, the best way to proceed is by covering all but the first trading day with a piece of cardboard or some other straight-edged implement. Then, exposing each day's price bar, trade volume and open-interest, mentally form conclusions about the technical significance of each session's trading symptoms.

Even knowledge of the general format of the overall chart pattern will prove to be of surprisingly small help in trying to trade the contract for a profit. Futures prices fluctuate constantly and sharply. Unless a trader is up to the task of rendering sensible judgments about events to come, he will lose. If he can draw reliable conclusions about the interacting forces that result in various configurations on his charts, he will profit from his speculations.

If the author has properly done his job of explanation and demonstration, you should now be able to put much of the information together and analyze a market from the technical point of view.

So, let's try it.

15

Computers Revisited

No development in information handling can even begin to compare with the incursions made by computers during the 18 years this book and its companion volume have been in print. While these amazing machines continue to carve out an ever-expanding niche for themselves in the processing of raw data and the crunching of statistical information, they have failed spectacularly in the area of telling us when to buy and sell commodities. Hope springs eternal, however, and even the most dismal track records are insufficient to dampen the ardor of those who constantly offer arcane trading programs to anyone who puts more faith into so-called computer science than he places in the art of personal evaluation based on study and observation.

Ancient alchemists were convinced that there had to be a way to turn lead into gold, and their patrons and supporters ran the gamut from monarchs to peasants. Indeed, there may be a way to transform the base metal into gold, but if so, it still eludes the investigators. The same possibility may apply to computers and commodity markets. Regardless of what the future may bring, the current state of computer technology is palpably unequal to the task of analyzing and trading commodity markets at a consistent profit. Having said this, little remains to be added—since any trading program that fails to produce consistent profitability points the way to speculative disaster. One need not sink several thousand dollars into electronic equipment to go broke trading. The most starry-eyed "plunger" can do this all by himself.

In spite of the latent gloom in the foregoing, a computer can be a useful tool in connection with trading activities, provided the user keeps its inherent limitations in mind. The matter was put into vivid and useful perspective by Joseph J. Kane, a pit trader of vast experience and insight:

> A trader should use a computer the same way the Navy uses radar. Its "blips" can alert a smart user to situations and opportunities that deserve some degree of attention and rational evaluation. Nobody knocks radar because it never sinks a ship all by itself. That isn't its job. All radar needs to do is help keep the skipper aware of what's going on around his position. A properly used computer can do the same thing for a trader; but it still requires somebody to make the decision to buy, or sell—or do nothing!

This volume and its companion piece, *Speculation in Commodity Contracts and Options*, point up a dozen or so elements that can bear importantly on price expectations in a given commodity or contract. These include:

Price.
Volume.
Open-interest.
Trading volume.
Trade mix between strong and weak hands.
Commodity Credit Corporation (CCC) stocks on hand.
Export orders.
Weather expectations.
Government crop reports.
Premiums and/or discounts to cash and nearby maturities.
Old-crop/new-crop balances.
Stocks in all positions.

A computer, a modem, and access to a commodity data bank that offers a full range of current and in-file information can keep a serious trader's fund of knowledge up-to-date, whether or not he elects to use all of it in any given trade decision. So if this kind of data support can be useful in upgrading trader decision making, why—it may well be asked—has no one succeeded in incorporating these data into a program matrix that will signal buy, sell, or wait, and be right more often than it's wrong? Answering the question is far more difficult than asking it.

The major difficulty appears to be that of assigning proper weights to the various considerations making up the computer equation (read program). In mid-August there is nothing more vital to the price of new-crop soybeans than temperatures and rainfall, whereas in March-April-May, weather is at most a secondary consideration. In view of this reality, any soybean trading program that includes a weather element is going to have to vary the weight given weather through the growing period. Weather can be crucial, but it is not a *constant*.

In a different situation, the major depressant for corn prices may be a disappointing pig farrowing report. Without a hog population to consume it, corn can quickly escalate into an overabundance—and low prices are sure to follow. Or a warm and wet December can keep the corn pickers out of the mucky fields, sending prices soaring.

Dozens or hundreds of such examples could be cited in the full complexity of planting, growing, harvesting, and transporting agricultural commodities to market. A computer program that gives proper attention to all of these market inputs—and seasonal permutations on them—is difficult to imagine and almost impossible to write.

In tacit recognition of the complexities to be dealt with in writing programs dealing with the full clutch of market inputs, most programmers follow the course of leaning most heavily on the matter of price itself. The hazards of doing this must now be apparent to anyone who has read this book.

A further flaw in most of the computer trading programs your author has examined is that they show a discernible upside bias. While this tends to make the results marginally more positive in ascending markets, the anomaly produces disasters when prices fall. While an upside or downside bias may be statistically discernible in given commodities or contracts at a selected point in time, to install bias in a computer program is simply absurd. Price-particle behavior supports no such thesis, even though most public traders tend to remain bulls through thick and thin.

In spite of all of these perceived shortcomings, coupled with what the most charitable appraisal would have to call undistinguished track records, computer software firms, consulting organizations, and private commodity advisers continue to offer trading programs that purport to substitute floppy disc hocus-pocus for rational decision making. The principal thing they all have in common is a serious dearth of demonstrable effectiveness over anything approaching a realistic time span.

One swallow doesn't make a spring, and a few months of profits in an ascending market, with an upside biased trading protocol, doesn't validate the system. Regardless of anything else, this verity should not be overlooked for a moment!

It must now be conceded that it *is possible* someone will eventually write a trading program that takes the guesswork and travail out of commodity speculation and always produces a profit. If this ever happens, of course, commodity trading will cease to be speculative, because it will have ceased to involve risk. Risk is the essential ingredient in speculation.

Beyond this, the sure-fire program will quickly permeate the industry, and its adherents will inexorably begin accumulating all of the speculative funds in the market. Trade will certainly dwindle when any element in the business demonstrates such a consistent advantage.

Should this happen, the modern alchemists will have—via computers—turned risk into certainty, and speculation into consistent and predictable profitability.

Can it happen? It isn't likely!

Thinking machines are a topic of intriguing discussion among members of the computer fraternity, but their appearance in even the simplest evaluative applications is not envisioned for decades at least. This seems to leave lots of time in which human practitioners will continue to meet the market on its own terms, analyze its behavior, and strive to render rational decisions about the risks it offers.

All things considered, it just might be easier to turn lead into gold than to reduce commodity price behavior to firmly established mathematical formulas.

But don't expect the alchemists to quit trying.

Glossary

Accumulate Buying by traders who expect to hold the contracts for a period of time. Building up a position over time.

Acreage Allotment The limitation on planted acreage established by the government for each farmer for basic crops.

Acreage Reserve A part of the farm program that applies to basic commodities, under which the farmer receives payment from the government for not planting part or all of his acreage allotment.

Actuals The physical commodities, as distinguished especially from futures contracts.

Afloat Grain which is loaded in vessels, in harbor, or in transit, but which has not reached its destination and been unloaded.

Arbitrage Simultaneous purchase of cash commodities or futures in one market against the sale of cash commodities or futures in the same or a different market to profit from a discrepancy in price. Also includes some aspects of hedging. *See* Spread.

Basis The spread or difference between the spot or cash price and the price of the near future. Basis may also be used to designate price differentials between cash and more distant futures, as well as different locations as specified.

Bear One who believes prices are too high and will decline.

Bear Market One where large supplies and/or poor demand cause a decline in price.

Bear-Spread A dual position involving two different contracts in a single commodity (e.g., May and September oats) in which the holder expects the nearest contract to lose in value, relative to the deferred. Since he wants the basis to widen, he will be short the near maturity and long the deferred. *See* Bull-Spread.

Bearish and Bullish When conditions suggest lower prices, a bearish situation is said to exist. If higher prices appear warranted, the situation is said to be bullish.

Bid A price offered subject, unless otherwise stated, to immediate acceptance for a specific amount of commodity.

Board Order or **Market-if-Touched (MIT) Order** An order to buy or sell when the market reaches a specific price. A board order to buy becomes a market order when the commodity sells (or is offered) at or below the order price. A board order to sell becomes a market order when the commodity sells (or is bid) at or above the order price.

Board of Trade (Chicago) Licensed contract commodity exchange located in Chicago, Illinois; affords facilities for futures trading, primarily in grains.

Bot Abbreviation for bought.

Break A sharp price decline.

Broad Tape A teletype reporting system that automatically prints out news, weather, markets, etc., as furnished from professional and government reporting services.

Broker An agent entrusted with the execution of an order. He may be employed in the office of the commission house that carries the account of a floor broker or pit broker who actually executes the order on the trading floor. *See* Customer's Man.

Brokerage The fee charged by a floor broker for execution of a transaction. The fee may be a flat amount or a percentage.

Brokerage House *See* Commission House.

Bucket, Bucketing The illegal practice of some brokers in accepting orders to buy or sell without executing such orders. Such a broker hopes to profit by pocketing the loss that a customer may experience when closing out the transaction. If the customer closes out at a profit, the bucketer expects to pay. The illegality lies in an agent's direct dealing with his principal without disclosing the fact.

Bulge A sharp price advance.

Bull One who believes prices are too low and will advance.

Bull Market One where small supplies and/or strong demand cause prices to rise.

Bull-Spread A dual position involving two different contracts in a single commodity (e.g., May and March bellies) in which the holder expects the nearer contract to gain in value, relative to the deferred. Since he wants the basis to narrow, he will be long the nearby and short the deferred. *See* Bear-Spread.

Buying Hedge Buying futures to hedge cash sales in present or future. *See* Hedging.

Buyer's Market A condition of the market in which there is an abundance of goods available and hence buyers can afford to be selective and may be able to buy at less than the price that had previously prevailed. *See* Seller's Market.

Buy in   To cover or liquidate a sale.

Buy on Close or Opening   To buy at the end or beginning of a session at a price within the closing or opening range.

Call   A period in which trading is conducted to establish the price for each futures month at a particular time, i.e., an opening or closing call.

   Buyer's Call   Purchase of a specified quantity of a specific grade of a commodity at a fixed number of points above or below a specified delivery month in futures, with the buyer being allowed a certain period of time within which to fix the price by either purchasing a futures for the account of the seller, or indicating to the seller when he wishes to price-fix.

   Seller's Call   The same as buyer's call with the difference that the seller has the right of determining the time of fix price.

Call   An option permitting its holder (who has paid a fee for the option) to call for a certain commodity futures contract or security at a fixed price in a stated quantity within a stated period. The broker is paid to bring the buyer and seller together. The buyer of this right to call expects the price of the commodity or security to rise so that he can call for it at a profit. If the price falls, the option will not be exercised. The reverse transaction is a Put. *See* Privilege.

Call Level   The price level at which additional margin money must be put up by the holder of an impaired open position.

Carload   For grains, may range from 1,400 to 2,500 bushels.

Carrying Costs   Those charges incurred in warehousing the actual commodity, generally including interest, insurance, and storage.

Cash Commodity   Physical merchandise; goods available for delivery immediately or within a designated period following sale; includes a commodity bought or sold to arrive.

Cash Forward   Sale of a cash commodity for delivery at a later date.

Cash Price   The current bid or offering price for a cash commodity of designated grade and for immediate delivery.

Cash Transaction   Purchase or sale of physical merchandise; can be in futures.

CCC   The Commodity Credit Corporation.

CEA   The Commodity Exchange Authority, Supplanted in 1974 by the Commodity Futures Trading Commission.

C & F   Cost and freight paid to port of destination.

CFTC   Commodity Futures Trading Commission.

Certified Stock   Stocks of a commodity that have been graded, have passed various tests and have been found to be of deliverable quality against futures contracts, which are stored at the delivery points and in warehouses designated regular for delivery by the Exchange.

Chart   Any of a variety of methods used to visually present economic data, for each of visual reference, mathematical analysis, etc.

Charter   An engagement of a vessel to a given destination at a fixed rate.

CIF   Cost, insurance, and freight paid (or included) to a port of destination.

Chicago Board of Trade   An organized commodity exchange which houses much of the world's futures trading in agricultural commodities.

Churning   Excessive trading in and out of commodity positions, when doing so has the main objective of generating commissions to the broker.

Clearances Total marine shipments from domestic and foreign ports.

Clearing Contracts The process of substituting principals to transactions through the operation of clearing associations, in order to simplify the settlement of accounts.

Clearing House The (separate) agency associated with a futures exchange through which futures contracts are offset or fulfilled and through which financial settlement is made. *See* Clearing Association.

Clearing Member A member of the Clearing House or Association. Each clearing member must also be a member of the Exchange. Each member of the Exchange, however, need not be a member of the Clearing Association; if not, his trades must be registered and settled through a clearing member.

Clearing Price *See* Settlement Price.

Close The period at the end of the trading session during which all trades are officially declared as having been executed "at or on the close." The closing range is the range of prices on trades made during this designated period.

COFO Commercially objectionable foreign odor.

Commission Fee charged by a broker for performance of specified market function.

Commission House A concern that buys or sells for the accounts of customers. Also called Brokerage House, sometimes Wire House.

Commodity An economic good of broad use and value, as distinguished from a service.

Commodity Credit Corporation (CCC) A wing of the U.S. Department of Agriculture which functions as the holding and marketing agency in connection with administered farm commodities.

Conservation Reserve The section of the Soil Bank Program calling for long-term contracts for the conversion of crop land into grasses, trees, and water conservation uses.

Consignment An unsold shipment of grain placed with a commission man who will offer it for sale.

Contract (1) A formal multilateral agreement between two (or more) parties in interest, which binds each to certain stipulated performances. In commodity trading, is usually synonymous with futures contract.

　　(2) A unit of the commodity being traded. Orders must specify the number of bushels to be bought and sold. *See* Round Lot; Job Lot.

Contract Grades The grades of a commodity listed in the rules of an exchange as those that can be used to deliver against a futures contract.

Contract Market An organized commodity futures market which qualifies under the Commodity Exchange Act.

Contract Maturity Relates to a given month: July, September, March, etc.

Controlled Commodity Commodities subject to federal regulation; listed in the Commodity Exchange Act. The list is comprised of domestically produced agricutural products.

Convergence or Convergence Principle "Cash price and the futures price will converge in the market location on the last day of trading in the expiring contract." The economic reality that makes this rule work is, on the last day of trading in the expiring futures contract, the futures contracts that have not been offset become physical commodities, and the obligations of settlement require the short to deliver the goods. The long must accept delivery and pay for the actuals in cash. Hence, on the last day of trading, the expiring contracts and the cash commodity become the same thing, sharing a common value in the given marketplace.

Core Sample *See* Sample.

Corner (1) To corner is to secure such relative control of a commodity or security that its price can be manipulated.

(2) In the extreme situation, obtaining more contracts requiring the delivery of commodities or securities than the quantity of such commodities or securities actually in existence.

Cost of Storage Rate charged for physical warehousing of a commodity; (may include in or out elevation charges). *See* Carrying Charge.

Country Elevator A grain elevator located in the immediate farming community to which farmers bring their grain for sale or storage, as distinct from a terminal elevator which is located at a major marketing center.

Country Price The price which prevails in an area removed from the central market (usually quoted as being "on" or "off" a designated futures price). *See* Basis.

Cover The purchase of futures to offset a previously established short position.

Crop Report Any of several forecasts made by both private and official sources. The major ones emanate from the Crop Reporting Board of the U.S.D.A. and equivalent bodies in Canada and elsewhere.

Crop Year Period used for statistical purposes, from the harvest of a crop to the corresponding period in following year. U.S. wheat crop year begins July 1 and ends June 30; cotton, August 1–July 31; varying dates for other commodities.

Crude Oil Oil which has undergone the first stage(s) of refinement.

Crush (Soybeans) The process which converts soybeans into meal and oil. Also, a term used to describe a particular spreading posture between soybeans and products.

Crush Spread In soybeans, the purchase of bean futures and simultaneous sale of an equivalent amount of meal and oil futures.

Current Delivery Means delivery during the present month.

Current Quotation The last price, bid, or offer on a designated futures, cash, etc.

Customers' Man An employee of a commission house, also called a broker, account executive, solicitor, or registered representative, who engages in soliciting or accepting and handling orders for the purchase or sale or any commodity for futures delivery on or subject to the rules of any contract market and who, in or in connection with such solicitations or acceptance of orders, accepts any money, securities, or property (or extends credit in lieu thereof) to margin any trades or contracts that result or may result therefrom. Must be licensed by C.F.T.C. when handling business in commodities traded on organized U.S. exchanges.

Daily Fluctuation Limits *See* Trading Limits.

Day Orders Those limited orders that are to be executed the day for which they are effective, or are automatically cancelled at the close of that day.

Day Trader   A speculator who carries no open positions overnight. He is usually a floor trader, a member of the exchange upon which he transacts most of his speculative business.

Deferred   Any contract which matures later than the nearby.

Deliverable Grades   *See* Contract Grades.

Delivery Month   The calendar month during which a futures contract matures.

Delivery Notice   The notification of delivery of the actual commodity on the contract, issued by the seller of the futures to the clearing house.

Delivery Points   Those locations designated by commodity exchanges at which a commodity covered by a futures contract may be delivered in fulfillment of the contract.

Delivery Price   The price fixed by the clearing house at which deliveries on futures are invoiced and also the price at which the futures contract is settled when deliveries are made.

Designated Markets   (By C.F.T.C.) *See* Contract Markets.

Differentials   The price difference between classes, grades, and locations of a given commodity or commodities.

Discount   Applied to cash prices that are below the future, or to deliveries at a lesser price than others (May at a discount under July) or to lesser prices caused by quality differences.

Discretionary Account   An account for which buying and selling orders can be placed by a broker or other person without the prior consent of the account owner for each such individual order, specific authorization having been previously granted by the account owner.

Distant or **Deferred Delivery**   Usually means one of the more distant months in which futures trading is taking place. *See* Cash Forward.

Dockage   *See* Foreign Material.

Ensilage   Chopped animal feed which is stored in bulk, usually in a moist condition.

Evening Up   Buying or selling to adjust or close out an open market position, also called offset.

Exchange of Spot or Cash Commodity for Futures   The simultaneous exchange of a specified quantity of a cash commodity for the equivalent quantities in futures, usually instituted between parties carrying opposite hedges in the same delivery month. Also known as "exchange for physical" or "against actuals," or as "giving up futures for cash." The exchange is usually made outside the pit.

Expeller Press   A machine used in soybean oil extraction.

Ex-pit Transaction   A trade made outside the exchange trading ring or pit which is legal in certain instances. It is primarily used in price-fixing transactions involving the purchase of cash commodities at a specified basis.

Ex-store   Selling term for commodities in warehouse.

Family Farm   In common usage, a nonspecializing farm of modest size which is presumed adequate to support a rural family.

FAQ   Fair average quality.

Farm Prices   The prices received by farmers for their products, as published by the U.S. Department of Agriculture; determined as of the 15th of each month.

Fibers   Raw materials, either natural or synthetic, from which a wide range of cloth and other products are fabricated.

Fill-or-Kill Order   A commodity order which demands immediate execution or cancellation.

First Notice Day   The first day on which notices of intentions to deliver actual commodities against futures market positions can be made or received. First notice day will vary with each commodity and exchange. It usually precedes the beginning of the delivery period.

Fixing the Price   The determination of the exact price at which a cash commodity will be invoiced after a call sale has previously been made based on a specified number of points on or off a specified futures month.

Flake   A soybean morsel from which the oil has been extracted.

Flash   Hand signals used by pit brokers.

Flat Price   Price on a single position; differing from spread price, which relates to a dual position.

Floor Broker   Any person who, in or surrounding any pit, ring, or other place provided by a contract market for the meeting of persons similarly engaged, executes for others any order for the purchase or sale of any commodity for future delivery on or subject to the rules of any contract market, and who for such services receives or accepts a prescribed fee or brokerage.

Floor Phone Man   An employee of a brokerage house who serves as the communication link between his firm's office and the brokers in the pits.

Floor Trader   An exchange member who executes his own trades by being personally present in the place provided for futures trading.

FOB   Free on board. Usually covers all delivery, inspection, and elevation costs involved in putting commodities on board whatever shipment conveyance is being used.

Forage   Natural pasture for livestock.

Foreign Material   Anything other than the designated commodity which is present in a lot.

Forward Shipment   A contract covering cash commodities to be shipped at some future specified date.

Free Balance   Margin funds on deposit with a broker, and which are not committed against existing open positions.

Free Market   A theoretical trade situation in which buying and selling decisions, production, and use judgments, etc., are unfettered by any uneconomic considerations such as price controls, export quotas, etc.

Free Supply   The quantity of a commodity available for commercial sale; does not include government held stocks.

Frost-Drop   Planned destruction of a designated portion of a growing crop for the purpose of restricting unwanted production.

Full Carrying Charge   (1) In market parlance, the cost involved in owning cash commodities over a period of time; including storage, insurance, and interest charges on borrowed working capital. (2) In futures, the cost, including all charges, of taking actual delivery in a given month, storing the commodity, and re-delivering against the next delivery month.

Fundamentalist   A market participant who relies principally on supply/demand considerations in his price forecasting activities; especially one who tends to give "technical" considerations small weight in his decisions.

Futures Commission Broker   *See* Customers' Man.

Futures Contract   Agreement to buy and receive or sell and deliver a commodity at a future date, with these distinguishing characteristics:
1. All trades in the same contract, such as a 5,000-bushel round lot of grain, have the same unit of trading.
2. The terms of all trades are standardized.
3. A position may be offset later by an opposite trade in the same contract.
4. Prices are determined by trades made by open outcry in the pit within the hours prescribed, or visually posted.
5. The contract has a basic grade, but more than one grade may be deliverable.
6. Delivery is required during designated periods.
7. The trades are cleared through a Clearing House daily. (Traders in cash or spot goods usually refer to sales for shipment or delivery in the futures as deferred or forward sales. Such sales, however, are not standardized as are futures contracts just described above.)

Futures Price   The price bid or offered for contract grade commodities, for delivery at a specified period in the future.

Futures Transaction   Purchase or sale of a futures contract; exchange of a futures position for the cash commodity.

Give-Up   This is a contract executed by one broker for the client of another broker, which the client orders turned over to the latter broker. Generally speaking, the order is sent over the leased wires of the first broker who collects a wire toll from the other broker for the use of his facilities.

Good-Till-Cancelled (GTC)   An order which will remain open for execution at any time in the future until the customer cancels it. For example: Sell one May soybean meal at $166.00 G.T.C.

Grain Futures Act   A federal statute that regulates trading in grain futures. Administered by the U.S.D.A. and the C.F.T.C.

Grains   For purposes of the Chicago Board of Trade: wheat, oats, rye, corn, and soybeans.

Gross Processing Margin   In the case of soybeans, GPM refers to the difference between the price paid for soybeans and the sum of prices received from the sale of oil and meat products after processing.

Growths   Description of commodity according to area of origin; either refer to country, district, or place of semimanufacture.

GTC   Good till cancelled. Usually refers to open orders to buy or sell at a fixed price.

Hard Spot   An interval of strength in the market, usually resulting from considerable buying.

Harden   A term indicating a slowly advancing market.

Heavy   This is applied to a market where there is an apparent number of selling orders overhanging the market without a corresponding amount of buying orders.

Hedger   Usually a dealer in physical commodities who holds positions in futures that are opposite his cash positions (e.g., long cash corn; short corn futures).

Hedging Briefly stated, hedging is the sale of futures against the physical commodity or its equivalent as protection against a price decline; or the purchase of futures against forward sales or anticipated requirements of the physical commodity as protection against a price advance.

Hedging on futures markets consists of buying (or selling) futures contracts in the amount to which one is long (or short) the actual commodity. Usually the futures transaction is nearly simultaneous with the spot transaction. Hedgers thereby fix or protect a carrying charge, a processing margin, etc. The futures hedge is thus a temporary substitute for an ordinary transaction which will occur later. Hedging also provides opportunities for added profit.

High The highest price posted within the designated period: day, contract, etc.

ICC Interstate Commerce Commission.

In Bond An inspected, sealed, and cleared shipment, actually in transit or scheduled for export.

Incentive Payment Plan The type of support program used for domestic clip wool, for example, in which a cash subsidy is paid to the wool grower based upon his selling price.

Initial Margin The amount of money required to bind performance on a newly established futures position. *See* Variation Margin.

Inspection In commodity marketing, an official evaluation procedure which results in a grade or class designation being assigned.

Inter-Commodity Spread A multiple position between two substitutive or related commodities (e.g., corn and oats).

Inter-Market Spread A multiple position between two exchanges (e.g., Minneapolis wheat/Kansas City wheat).

International Wheat Agreement A multigovernment treaty arrangement which fixes the price of this commodity in international trade between the participating nations.

Intra-Market Spread A multiple position between commodities traded on a single exchange (e.g., Chicago soybeans/Chicago soybean oil).

Inverted Market A futures market in which the nearer months are selling at premiums to the more distant months; hence, a market displaying inverse carrying charges. These price relationships are characteristic of situations in which supplies are currently in shortage.

Investor One who commits capital to a given business proposition, with his hopes for return tied exclusively to interest, dividends, rent, etc.

Invisible Supply Uncounted stocks in the hands of wholesalers, manufacturers, and producers that cannot be identified accurately; stocks outside commercial channels, but available for commerce.

Job Lot A unit of trading smaller than the regular round lot, usually, in grains, 1,000 or 2,000 bushels.

Jumped Stop *See* Stop-Loss Order.

Key Reversal A trading event in which price peaks or plummets as a result of buying by squeezed shorts offsetting, or squeezed longs selling out in the face of losses. This desperation buying or selling generates unusually high volume ordinarily, after which (with the disadvantaged traders' requirements satisfied) trade slows and price moves in the opposite direction.

Open-interest may be significantly reduced by the reversal trading, or it may not be.

Land-Bank Program   A government program that seeks to manage agricultural production by taking land out of use or returning it to use, depending on projected needs.

Last Trading Day   The day on which trading ceases for a particular delivery month. All contracts that have not been offset by the end of trading on that day must thereafter be settled by delivery of the actual physical commodity, or by agreement. *See* Wash Sales.

Leverage   In speculation, the increased power of money committed in a situation involving margin (which is less than the total value of the property covered in the commitment).

Life of Delivery or Contract   The period between the beginning of trading in a particular future to the expiration of that future.

Limit-Only   In trading, the definite price stated by a customer to a broker restricting the execution of an order to buy for not more than, or to sell for not less than, the stated price.

Limit (up or down)   The maximum price advance or decline from the previous day's settlement price permitted in one trading session by the rules of the exchange.

Limited Order   One in which the client sets a limit on the price, as contrasted with a market order.

Liquidation   The closing out of a long position. It is also sometimes used to denote closing out a short position, but this is more often referred to as covering.

Liquidating Market   One in which the predominant feature is longs selling their holdings.

Liquidity (Market)   Refers to the demonstrated or presumed ability of a trading situation to accommodate buyers and sellers with a minimum relative distortion of price, on the basis of insufficient opposites to handle proffered trades efficiently. Open-interest tends to be a useful indication of liquidity, with large interest being productive of good liquidity, and small interest reflecting the probability of limited liquidity.

Loan Price   The statutory price at which growers may obtain crop loans from the government.

Loan Program   The primary means of government price support in which the government lends money to the farmer at a preannounced price schedule with the farmer's crop as collateral. The primary method by which the government acquires stocks of agricultural commodities. *See* Non-Recourse Loans.

Long Hedge   The purchase of futures against sales of cash (usually for deferred delivery).

Long the Basis   This is said of one who has bought cash or spot goods and has hedged them with sales of the futures. He has therefore bought at a certain basis on or off futures and hopes to sell at a better basis with the futures for a profit. *See* Hedging.

Long-Squeeze   A market situation in which longs are forced to liquidate in the face of falling prices.

Long-Term   A period of time adequate to permit unfolding of major trends in production, consumption, utility patterns, etc.

Low   The lowest price posted within the designated period: day, contract, etc.

Maintenance Margin   Same as Variation Margin.

Margin   The amount deposited by buyers and sellers of futures to insure performance on contract commitments; serves as a performance bond rather than a down payment.

Margin Call   A request to deposit either the original margin at the time of the transaction, or to restore the guarantee to maintenance margin levels required for the duration of the time the contract is held.

Margin Funds   Moneys on deposit with a broker (or the clearing house) to bind performance on commodity futures positions.

Margin of Cultivation, Extensive   The situation in which unit doses of labor and capital applied to less and less productive land finally reach land of such poor quality that the product just pays for the labor and capital.

Market Order or **Board Order**   An order to buy or sell when the market reaches a specified point. A board order to buy becomes a market order when the commodity sells (or is offered) at or below the order price. A board order to sell becomes a market order when the commodity sells (or is bid) at or above the order price.

Market Price   The price that prevails in the central market, as compared to country price.

Market Psychology   The composite attitude of bulls and bears, especially as it relates to prospects for price behavior.

Market Technician   Any of a variety of traders and/or analysts who attempt to appraise the present balance between buyers and sellers, as concerns market influences, and, from such analyses, project relative strengths and weaknesses in terms of potentials for price effects in the near-term period.

Market Trend   General direction of prices without regard to short-term fluctuations.

Marketing Quota   A federally enforced restriction on the amount of a commodity that a producer is permitted to sell. Usually conforms to the quantity of wheat, corn, etc., the farmer can grow on his acreage allotment.

Marketplace   Broadly, the area in which buyers and sellers deal in selected goods and in which transportation, exchange of information, common currency, and methods of trade are sufficiently uniform to create a more or less distinct economic arena.

Maturity   The period within which a futures contract can be settled by delivery of the actual commodity; the period between first notice day and last trading day. Often used as a synonym for contract (e.g., July corn maturity, December wheat maturity, etc.).

Medium-Range   A period of time sufficient to accommodate fundamental changes in supply/demand balance. Usually one crop year or less.

Members' Rate   The commission charge for the execution of an order for a person who is a member of and thereby has a seat on the exchange. It is less than the commission charged to a customer who does not have a seat on the exchange.

Moving Average Price   A composite of individual prices over a given period of time. Often employed by chartists to define a price trend, as compared to short-term price fluctuations.

Nearby   The futures contract which is nearest to maturity.

Nearby Delivery   The nearest traded contract month.

Negative Carrying Charge   *See* Inverted Market.

Negotiable Warehouse Receipt   Document issued by a regular warehouse that guarantees existence and grade of commodity held in store. Transfer of ownership can be accomplished by endorsement of the warehouse receipt.

Net Position   The difference between the open contracts long and the open contracts short, held in any one commodity.

New Crop   The projected harvest.

Nominal Price   A declared price for a futures month. Used at times to designate a closing price when no trading has taken place in that particular contract during the final few minutes of the trading session. It is usually the average between the bid and the asked prices.

Non-Recourse Loans   A loan under the U.S. agricultural program to farmers on the security of surplus crops that are delivered to the government and held off the market. The loan must be liquidated as provided by the government's program, but the government has no recourse against the farmer for a deficiency if the security fails to bring the amount of the loan.

Notice Day   Any day on which notices of intent to deliver on futures contracts may be issued.

Notice of Intention to Deliver   A document furnished by a short-seller indicating his intention to fulfill his contract obligation by delivering cash merchandise.

OCO   One cancels other, in which filling of one order cancels customer's alternative order.

Off   In quoting the basis, the number of points the cash price will be under a specified futures price. Example: 20 points off December.

Off the Board   Close of trading in a maturing contract.

Offer   An indication of willingness to sell at a given price. (Opposite of bid.)

Official Inspection   *See* Inspection.

Offset   Usually the liquidation of a long or short futures position by an equal and opposite futures transaction.

Oils   In commodity trading, usually includes soybean oil, cottonseed oil, olive oil, rapeseed oil, safflower oil, and other edible fats that are broadly substitutive.

Old Crop   The past harvest.

Omnibus Account   An account carried by one futures commission merchant with another, in which the transactions of two or more persons are combined rather than designated separately and the identity of individual accounts is not disclosed.

On   In quoting the basis, the number of points the cash commodity is above a specified futures month. Example: 20 points on December.

On-Consignment Grain   Usually refers to grain conveyed to a broker for sale in the cash market.

On the Close   The last few (two or three) minutes of each trading session (varies).

On the Open   The initial two or three minutes of trading in each session (varies).

Open Contract   Contracts which have been bought or sold, without the transactions having been completed by subsequent sale or re-purchase or actual delivery or receipt of the commodity.

Open-Interest   The total of unfilled or unsatisfied contracts on one side of the market. (In any one delivery month, the short interest always equals the long interest, since the total number of contracts sold must equal the total number bought.)

Open-Order   *See* Good-Till-Cancelled.

Open Outcry   Required method of registering all bids and offers in the pits.

Opening Bell, Closing Bell   The signal that begins and ends each trading session on each exchange.

Opening Range–Closing Range   In open auction with many buyers and sellers, commodities are often traded at several prices at the opening or close of the market. Buying or selling orders at the opening might be filled at any point within such a price range.

Option   A term sometimes erroneously applied to a futures contract. It may refer to a specific delivery month, as "the July option." Puts and Calls or privileges, which are now legal in regulated commodity exchanges, are true options, entailing no delivery obligation. Futures contracts are not options.

Original Margin   The margin needed to cover a specific new position.

Over-Fill   A trading error in which an excessive purchase or sale is made.

Oversold or **Overbought Markets**   When the specultive long interest has been drastically reduced and the speculative short interest increases, actually or relatively, a market is said to be oversold. At such times, sharp rallies often materialize. On the other hand, when the speculative long-interest has increased rapidly and the speculative short interest decreases sharply, a market is said to be overbought. At such times, the market is often in a position to decline sharply.

Oversupply   A market situation in which available commodities exceed demonstrated demand. Result is usually seen in lowering prices. *See* Undersupply.

Paper Losses   The total extent of impairment in the margin deposited against an open position.

Paper Profit   The profit that might be realized if the open contracts were liquidated as of a certain time or at a certain price. Margin requirements are adjusted according to paper profits, hence they are to some extent real.

Paper-Trading   A method by which market trading can be simulated for purposes of gaining experience and background information in the activities concerned.

Parity   (A theoretically equal relationship between commodity prices and all other prices.) Equality of relationship. Specifically, in farm program legislation, parity is defined in such a manner that the purchasing power of a unit of the commodity is maintained at the level prevailing during some earlier historical base period.

Pits   Designated locations on the trading floor where futures trading takes place in particular commodities.

Point   The minimum price fluctuation in futures. It is equal to 1/100 of one cent in most futures traded in decimal units.

Position   To be either long or short in the market.

Position Limit   The maximum number of contracts one can hold open under the rules of the C.F.T.C.

Position Trader   One who holds a net long or short position open overnight or longer, as contrasted to a day trader, a spreader, or a scalper.

Posted, on the Board   The point at which a given price, bid, or offer is made known to the trade.

Premium   The excess in price at which one delivery or quality of goods is selling over the value of another delivery or quality, or the price relationship between cash and futures.

Price Averaging   The practice of adding to losing positions on the theory of averaging selling price upward, or buying price downward.

Price Dip   A sharp price drop.

Price Fix   *See* Fixing the Price.

Price Plateau   An area of congestion in trade where buying and selling forces remain in close balance; and this creates a sideways pattern in a bar chart.

Price Rationing   The action of higher prices in discouraging consumption and encouraging production, and lower prices in encouraging consumption and discouraging production.

Price Spread   Price difference between commodities, maturities, or geographical locations.

Primary Market   The centers to which the producers bring their goods for sale, such as country grain elevators.

Private Wire   A leased or owned communication link for the exclusive use of a single individual or brokerage house.

Privilege   The term often used to identify an option contract. *See* Call, Put.

Professional Speculator   Anyone who voluntarily owns valuable property over time or assumes the risks of such ownership in the hope of earning a profit through price change.

Program Trading   Pursuit of a speculative program that calls for successive steps at designated price intervals, especially as the practice relates to pyramiding.

Public Elevators   Grain storage facilities in which space is rented out to whoever wishes to pay for it; where grain is stored in bulk. These are licensed and regulated by the state and/or federal government, and may also be approved as regular for delivery on an organized commodity exchange.

Public Speculator   A private person who trades in futures contracts through a brokerage house.

Purchase Agreement   A form of government price support in which the government agrees to buy commodities from a farmer at a specified time at a designated loan price.

Purchase and Sales Statement (abbreviated P&S)   A statement sent by a commission merchant to a customer when his futures position has changed. It shows the amount involved, the prices at which the position was acquired and closed out, the gross profit or loss, the commission charges, and the net profit or loss on the transaction.

Puts   An option permitting its holder to sell a certain commodity or futures contract at a fixed price, and within a stated period. Such a right is purchased for a fee (premium) paid the one who agrees to accept the goods if they are offered. The buyer of this right to sell expects the price of the commodity to fall so that he can deliver the commodity (fill the put) at a profit.

If the price rises, the option need not be exercised. The reverse transaction is a call. *See* Privileges.

Pyramiding   Using the profits on a previously established position as margin for adding to that position.

Quick Order   *See* Fill-or-Kill Order.

Quotations   The changing prices on cash and futures.

Range   The difference between the highest and lowest prices recorded during a specified trading period.

Reaction   Downward tendency in prices following an advance.

Realizing   Taking profits.

Recovery   Advance after a decline.

Registered Representative   *See* Customers' Man.

Regulated Commodities   Those commodities over which the Commodity Futures Trading Commission has supervision are known as regulated. This does not mean that the prices are controlled. The C.F.T.C. simply concerns itself with the orderly operation of the futures market and at times investigates abnormal price movements. Under the Commodities Exchange Act, approved June 15, 1936, as amended, definite regulations were established providing for the safeguarding of customers' money deposited as margin. Commodities currently supervised by the C.F.T.C. include wheat, cotton, corn, rice, oats, barley, rye, flaxseed, grain sorghums, bran, shorts, middlings, butter, eggs, potatoes, onions, wool tops, grease wool, lard, tallow, soybean oil, cottonseed meal, cottonsed oil, cottonseed, peanuts, soybeans, soybean meal, livestock, livestock products, peanut oil, frozen concentrated orange juice, heating oil, lumber, financial instruments, currencies, and precious metals.

Resting Order   Instructions to buy at a figure below the present market price or sell at a figure above it.

Restricted Stocks   Loan stocks, etc. A separate segregation which, during recent years of control, has been applied to supplies officially off the market for a definite or indefinite period.

Reversal Point   The point on a price chart at which prices have reversed themselves in the past, and/or in the future are expected to do so.

Ring   *See* Pit.

Round Lot   A full contract as opposed to the smaller job lot. Round lots of grain are 5,000 bushels.

Round Turn   The completion of both a purchase and an off-setting sale or vice versa.

Rules   The regulations governing trading established by each exchange.

Sample   In marketing, one or more units of a product given free (or sold at a price far below market) in order to induce prospective buyers to give it a trial, or to enable them to determine its characteristics by inspection or analysis.

Sample Grade   In commodities (except grains), usually the lowest quality acceptable for delivery in settlement of a futures contract.

Sampling   In statistics and research, a sampling is an approximation of the nature or magnitude of some characteristics of a universe, arrived at through actual measurement of some of the individual units or elements of that universe called a sample, which may be chosen at random or by other criteria.

Scalper A speculator operating on the trading floor who provides market liquidity by buying and selling rapidly, with small profits or losses, and who holds his position for a short time. Typically, a scalper stands ready to buy at a fraction below the last transaction price and to sell at a fraction above.

Securities The various classes of stocks which are issued by corporations and which represent equity ownership in the issuing firms.

Seller's Market A condition of the market in which there is a scarcity of goods available, and hence sellers can obtain better conditions of sale or higher prices.

Seller's Option The right of a seller to select, within the limits prescribed by a contract, the quality of the commodity delivered and the time and place of delivery.

Selling Hedge *See* Hedging.

Settlement Price The daily price at which the clearing house clears all the day's trades; also a price which may be established by the exchange to settle contracts unliquidated because of acts of God, such as floods, market congestion, or other causes.

Short The selling side of an open futures contract; also refers to a trader whose net position shows an excess of open sales over open purchases.

Short Hedge Sales of futures against the purchase of cash.

Short of the Basis This is said of a person or firm who has sold cash or spot goods and has hedged them with purchases of futures. He has therefore sold at a certain basis and expects to buy back at a better basis for a profit.

Short Squeeze A sharp run-up of prices which forces shorts to offset (buy back open positions) in order to avoid larger losses.

Soften A slowly declining market price.

Soil Bank A government program designated to take farmland out of productive use. The government pays the farmer to not plant crops, but instead, to plant the land in grass or trees.

Sold Out Market A market in which liquidation of weakly held contracts has largely been completed and such offerings have become scarce.

Solicitor A member or nonmember who solicits business for a member.

Speculation The owning of valuable property over time (or assumption of the risks of such ownership) in the hope of profiting from a change in market value.

Speculative Capital The portion of a speculator's assets that have been earmarked for use in the risk market.

Speculative Interval The period of time left in the life of a contract during which it can be traded; or the period of time which largely governs speculative activities of public speculators, position traders, day traders, and scalpers.

Speculator (Professional) One who voluntarily deals in physical property (or risks) and relies on price change to produce a profit (risk premium) for him.

Spot Commodity Goods available for immediate delivery following sale; improperly used to include a commodity bought or sold "to arrive." Also called Actuals. *See* Cash Commodity.

Spot Price The price at which a physical commodity is selling at a given time and place.

Spread or **Straddle** These terms mean the same thing, but in practice the grain trade uses the term *spread*, whereas other commodity interests use the term *straddle*. A spread may be defined as the purchase of one futures against the sale of another future of the same commodity or a different commodity in the same or different markets. C.F.T.C. defines spreading only in terms of the same commodity, whereas exchanges define it to include different but related commodities.

Stipulation of Compliance In commodity usage, formal assurance on the part of an individual or firm that an administrative request or order from C.F.T.C. or other regulative body will be followed.

Stock Specialist Securities market principal who is required to buy or sell whenever public offerings to buy or sell are inadequate to maintain an orderly market.

Stockpile Commodities Commodities that are accumulated and held under government programs: gold, wheat, butter, etc.

Stop-Order or **Stop-Loss Order** An order entered to buy or sell when the market reaches a specified point. A stop order to buy becomes a market order when the commodity sells (or is bid) at or above the stop price. A stop order to sell becomes a market order when the commodity sells (or is offered) at or below the stop price. The purpose of a stop-loss order is to limit losses or protect a profit.

Straddle *See* Spread.

Strong Hands Usually refers to commercial hedgers and well-financed professional speculators who are hard to shake loose from an established market posture.

Subsidy A sum of money offered by government to assist in the establishment or support of an enterprise or program which is considered to be in the public interest.

Supply Demand Balance The known or estimated adequacy of supplies in light of known or projected needs. Also called supply/demand equilibrium.

Switch The liquidation of a position in one future of a commodity and the simultaneous reinstatement of such positions in another future of the same commodity. It may be done at market or at a specified difference.

Tape Trader A speculator who follows current market prices somewhat constantly on a ticker or some other quotation device.

Technical Rally (or Decline) A price movement resulting from conditions developing within the futures market itself and not dependent on outside supply and demand factors. These conditions would include changes in the open interest, volume, degree of recent price movement, and approach of first notice day.

Tender Delivery against a short futures position.

Terminal Elevator A grain storage facility at one of the major centers of agricultural product marketing.

Ticker Tape A stock or commodity quotation system. *See* Broad Tape.

Time-Limit Order An order to buy or sell when time of day is the controlling consideration.

Track-Country-Station   Usually involves a price designation; indicates the cost of a given commodity loaded in rail car and ready for shipment from an interior location.

Trading Limit   In virtually all North American commodity contracts, there is a maximum price change permitted for a single session. These limits vary in the different markets. After prices have advanced or declined to the permissible daily limits, trading automatically ceases unless, of course, offers appear at the permissible upper trading limit or bids appear at the permissible lower limit.

Trading Range   The interval between the highest and lowest price on a given contract or classification of goods in a designated period: daily, weekly, life-of-contract, etc.

Trading Rules   Usually refers to the rules and regulations of an organized exchange, which govern activities of both members and nonmembers who trade in the particular market.

Trading Session   The period from the opening to the close on a single day.

Transfer Notice or Delivery Notice   A written announcement issued by a seller signifying his intention of making delivery in fulfillment of a futures contract. The recipient of the notice may make a sale of the future and transfer the notice within a specified time to another party on some exchanges directly, and on others through the clearing association. The last recipient takes delivery of the commodity tendered. Notices on some exchanges are not transferable.

Trend   The direction in which prices are moving.

Trier   *See* Sample.

Under-Fill   A trading error in which a smaller than intended purchase or sale is made.

Undersupply   A situation in which demand for a commodity exceeds physical stocks offered for sale in the market. Result is usually seen in rising prices. *See* Oversupply.

U.S.D.A.   United States Department of Agriculture.

Variation Margin   The amount of money required to be kept constantly on deposit throughout the period a futures position remains open, as a binder of performance on the contract.

Variation Margin Call   A request for additional margin funds as collateral, occasioned by negative price movement against the held position.

Visible Supply   The amount of a particular commodity in store at loading centers. In the grain markets, the total stock of grain in store in public and some private elevators in the principal primary markets, plus certain stock afloat.

Volume of Trading   The purchases and sales of a commodity future during a specified period. Inasmuch as purchases equal sales, only one side is shown in published reports.

Warehouse Receipt   A document evidencing possession by a warehouseman (licensed under the U.S. Warehouse Act, or under the laws of a state) of the commodity named in the receipt. Warehouse receipts, to be tenderable on future contracts, must be negotiable receipts covering commodities in warehouses recognized for delivery purposes by the exchange on which such futures contracts are traded.

Wash Sales   Fictitious transactions contrived by two or more brokers in order to create a market price for a security or for tax evasion. It may also consist of two or more outside operators who match their orders for purchase and sale so that a seeming market activity is given to stock. Illegal and prohibited by law and by the exchanges. Tax law usually considers a repurchase within 30 days at a loss to be a wash sale. In commodity futures, contracts left open after the last day of trading may be settled by wash sales in lieu of delivery.

Weak Hands   Usually refers to poorly capitalized public traders who cannot be expected to stick to their guns in the face of adverse price movement.

Weather Market   A market characterized by erratic price behavior based largely on weather developments or weather prospects, vis-á-vis particular growing crops, delivery conditions, etc.

Wire House   Refers to a commission house with branch offices connected by telephone, teletype, telegraph, or cable.

World Market   Total global supply and demand, subject to such trading barriers as are erected by governments from time to time.

Index

MP